FAITH THAT WORKS

A TOPICAL STUDY ON THE BOOK OF JAMES

ANNE FORTENBERRY

HANNIBAL BOOKS
www.hannibalbooks.com

Published by
Hannibal Books
PO Box 461592
Garland, Texas 75046-1592
Copyright Anne Fortenberry 2009
All Rights Reserved
Printed in the United States of America

Cover design by Dennis Davidson
Except where otherwise indicated, all Scripture taken from the
New Living Translation
Wheaton, IL: Tyndale House Publishers (1996)
ISBN 978-1-934749-49-4
Library of Congress Control Number: 2009925199

TO ORDER ADDITIONAL COPIES FOR $15.95 EACH (ADD $4.00 SHIP-
PING FOR FIRST BOOK, $.50 FOR EACH ADDITIONAL BOOK) CONTACT
Hannibal Books
PO Box 461592
Garland, TX 75046-1592
www.hannibalbooks.com
800-747-0738 (toll free)

Acknowledgements

Sincere appreciation, gratitude, and heartfelt thanks are extended to the following persons whose assistance made this study possible—

• My Heavenly Father, who guided my thoughts and prayers as I wrote this study. I was constantly amazed at how everything just "fell into place"—the outline, content, Scripture, and even my personal life experiences. Thank You, Father!

• My precious husband, Archie, who not only is my life partner of 43 years as well as my best friend, he also is my encourager and first editor. Thank you, Honey!

• My first ladies group (the "Awesome 39"), who supported and encouraged me throughout this entire process to include having this study published. Wow! They even patiently put up with my tears as we struggled together to understand God's Word and to grow closer to our Heavenly Father. Two of these precious ladies, whom I cannot name because of the nature of their work, were instrumental in asking me to write this study. One of these ladies served as my second editor. With all my heart I thank each of you!

• Last but certainly not least, my publishers, Louis and Kay Moore with Hannibal Books, who tirelessly did the final editing on this study as well as led me through this entire publication process. I truly appreciate your answering all my questions which probably at times seemed rather useless and even unwise. Thank you for your guidance and patience!

What others are saying about this study:

God used this study to pinpoint certain areas in my life that needed change/growth.

Cynthia, a teacher from America

I am glad for the challenge that Anne gave me to make my faith one that works. I appreciate her honesty and transparency about her own faith walk.

Robin, a school principal and nurse from America serving in the Middle East

Anne challenges us to think about the real meaning of the passage and how to apply it.

Linda, a professional counselor from America serving in the Middle East

This study helped me learn how to apply a workable faith. God bless the author, for she has a loving, sincere heart full of experiences.

Hala, a national woman born and reared in the Middle East

Anne has put in a lot of effort for a good in-depth study of James. She speaks from her own life, which makes us realize that as Christians we are able to overcome through Christ.

Rupa, a teacher from India who is in the Middle East to serve with her family

Foreword

We have no lack of Bible-study materials available to those seeking to understand and apply God's Word to our lives and Christian growth. Such materials cover the spectrum between highly technical, scholarly approaches and shallow overviews that bring no new insights or practical help to the reader.

Dr. Anne Fortenberry's study of the Book of James, *Faith that Works*, is an inspiring and refreshing approach to an interactive Bible study that will strengthen participants' faith, enrich their walk with the Lord, and challenge them to practical application of well-known spiritual principles.

Dr. Fortenberry uses a unique style of communication to lead the reader through a pattern of discovery that grows out of the Word itself. As a missionary and educator, she reveals fresh insights through a pattern of inductive questions. One feels an intimate relationship with the author as if chatting over a cup of coffee as she injects expressions of "Wow!" or *"Hmmm"* to challenging precepts.

Her research is thorough and comprehensive. A stronger faith lived out in practical ways through relationships and ministry will be the result for those engaging in this delightful study of the Book of James.

Jerry Rankin, President
International Mission Board, SBC

Contents

Topics	Scripture Reference	Page
Introduction		7
Overview		9
Session Worksheet		12
Week 1		
Tests of Faith	1:1-18	15
Characteristics of Faith		
Faith Obeys the Word	1:19-27	34
Week 2		
Faith Removes Partiality	2:1-13	38
Week 3		
Faith Confirms Itself by Action	2:14-26	59
Week 4		
Faith Controls the Tongue	3:1-12	76
Week 5		
Faith Produces Wisdom	3:13-18	97
Week 6		
Faith Produces Humility	4:1-12	121
Week 7		
Faith Produces Trust in God	4:13-5:6	144
Week 8		
Victories of Faith		
Faith Waits Patiently	5:7-12	167
Week 9		
Faith Prays Faithfully	5:13-20	190
Translations		216
Bibliography		217
Appendix Charts, Illustrations, Evaluation		218

Introduction

This process began when I had to reconcile in my mind just who the author of James really was; that took some time. After I accepted the fact that the author of this book is James, the half-brother of my Lord and Savior, Jesus, my entire perspective changed. For one minute can you imagine waking up in the same household with Jesus? Can you imagine eating meals with Jesus, playing with Jesus, maybe even arguing with Jesus? WOW!

Then I realized that James probably doesn't believe who his half-brother, Jesus, really is until after Jesus' crucifixion. You may remember that James is present with the 11 disciples when Jesus appears before them after His resurrection (1 Cor. 15:7; Luke 24:33; Mark 16:13). Also, James is present along with the disciples and praying in one accord when the Holy Spirit descends to them (Acts 1:14 and 2:1-4). How awesome is that? From history we also know that James goes on to become one of leaders in the Jerusalem church. Clearly James has a life-changing experience with Jesus, because we see he begins his letter by calling himself a *slave* of the Lord Jesus Christ. Not one time does he refer to Jesus as his half-brother! In fact James speaks of Jesus as *the* Lord Jesus. Isn't that beautiful?

That is what Jesus does in our lives. He makes a real difference. He changes our hearts—our entire belief system—our very lives, if we let Him.

Faith that Works is more than a topical Bible study. It is a guidebook to Christian living that will enable you to discover how to put your faith into action. Hopefully by the end of this journey you will have a stronger faith in our Heavenly Father, be prepared to meet life's challenges, and know He is always present to walk with you every day of your life.

Join me now as we study this wonderful Book of James. You will discover that it is only five chapters long with a total of 108 verses, but it is packed with awe-inspiring truths. You will learn that the central theme is faith and how to put that faith into action. In this study you will find an overview plus nine weekly lessons; each lesson is divided into five daily studies.

The introductory overview week is designed to give you some background information on the person of James. You will discover why he wrote this book and why this is so important in our spiritual growth as Christians. The introductory overview week will conclude with a Session Worksheet for you to prepare and bring to your first group meeting. Reading through the introduction and overview and preparing your worksheet before your first group meeting will help.

As you study the lessons, please take your time and seriously think about what God may be saying to you. As you work through the study, read the background verses listed at the top of each day's lesson, and really digest God's Word. The questions are designated by the heart symbol (♥) and are designed to help you think about what you have just read. Answer them honestly. Remember, this is an interactive study; don't be afraid to apply it personally to your life.

What would a Bible Study be without God's Truths that speak to our heart? Therefore, you will find these Heart Truths in a box on the first page of each lesson and also listed on the introductory page each week. These Heart Truths are designated by the cross symbol (†) and designed to encourage you to put God's Word to memory. These verses are simply suggestions; instead, you may choose any verse that God places on your heart to commit to memory. However, to obey God's Word, don't merely read it but also memorize and meditate on it. If you are to build your life on His Word, then build His Word into your life. Scripture says that to be able to make yourself approved by God (2 Tim. 2:15), hide His Word in your heart, that you will not sin against Him (Ps. 119:11). It also says to always be ready to speak out boldly for Jesus (Phil. 1:20 LB).

At the end of each day's lesson, I ask for Your Thoughts. This will be your time to write down any of your questions or comments about the study and bring them to the weekly group time. It is also designed for you to jot down your prayer requests and/or answers to prayer that you may like to share. This is your Bible Study; you might like to write your notes in your book or in your spiritual journal. The choice is yours. However, I pray that by responding to Your Thoughts, at the end of this study you will have grown closer in your relationship with our Heavenly Father as well as see many answers to your prayers.

To grow in our relationship with our Heavenly Father we need each other. Therefore weekly group times will consist not only of discussing questions listed in your Bible study but also in our sharing with each other. We will review what you have covered during the previous week and discuss how to apply the faith concepts to your daily life. A spiritual journey is healthier when shared, so let me encourage you as you take this journey to get involved with a group.

Most of all, I ask that you pray before you begin each study and ask our Heavenly Father for His guidance and discernment as you prepare your lessons. Please know I am not an authority on His Holy Word; I am only His servant who is willing to share. My prayer for you during this study is threefold:

1. That our Heavenly Father will speak to you through His Word and through the presence of His Holy Spirit.
2. That you will grow a minimum of one step higher in your relationship with the Father and in your commitment to our Lord Jesus.
3. That you will apply the principles found in this Bible study and turn your faith into actions in your daily life.

I challenge you to commit to the Lord and yourself to give about 30 minutes of your time each day to reading and studying His Word. You will not regret it.

Someone once said, "Move over fear; here comes faith"—a *Faith that Works*! Thank you for joining me.

Overview

James the Author

The name *James*, or in the Greek, *Iakobos*, is a form of the Hebrew name for *Jacob*. *James* was a common name in the first century as well as today. Four men in the New Testament have the name of *James*: (1) James, the father of Judas (not Iscariot) is mentioned twice (Luke 6:16 and Acts 1:13). (2) James, the son of Alphaeus and sometimes called *James the Less*, is one of the 12 disciples. However, past the four gospels he is not mentioned again. Some have tried to make him to be the author, but this is difficult to reconcile with the gospel accounts. (3) James, the son of Zebedee and brother of John, is one of Jesus' intimate disciples but is martyred in AD 44 (Acts 12:2), which makes unlikely the option that he wrote this book. (4) And, James, the Lord's half brother (Mt. 13:55; Mark 6:3).

As evidenced by Scripture, tradition points to James, the Lord's half brother, as the author because of these reasons: (1) James is one of the pillars in the Jerusalem church. (2) The language found in this book is similar to the language found in the letter drafted to the churches from the Jerusalem Council (Acts 15:23-29). (e.g., the word, *chairein*, meaning "greeting", is found only in Acts and James.) (3) The Jewish character of this book stresses the law along with the evident influence of the 15 indirect references to the Sermon on the Mount (Jas. 4:11, 12; 5:12). (See Appendix, Chart 1: Comparing James to the Sermon on the Mount, page 218.)

James the Person

What do we know about James the person? We know that he is the offspring of Mary and Joseph after the birth of Jesus. This would make him the half-brother of Jesus (Mt. 1:24, 25). He may not have accepted the claims of Jesus until Jesus, after His resurrection, appears to him (Luke 24:33; Mark 16:13). James and his brothers are among the believers who wait for the arrival of the Holy Spirit on the day of Pentecost (Acts 1:14). Shortly thereafter, James becomes an acknowledged leader of the Jerusalem church (Acts 12:17; Gal. 2:9, 12) and is the central figure in the Jerusalem Council (Acts 15). After Paul's third missionary journey, James observes the Jewish law as a testimony to other Jews (Acts 21:18-25). Tradition stresses his Jewish piety and his role in bringing others to an understanding of Jesus as the Messiah. According to the *Chronicles of Biblical Christianity,* James suffers a violent martyr's death not long before the fall of Jerusalem. Josephus records the following in AD 62, "When Ananus was made High Priest he had James, the half-brother of Jesus, cast from a pinnacle of the Temple, showered with stones and finally his skull smashed and his brains beaten out with a fuller's club. He is buried on the Mount of Olives." Tradition has it that James spent so much time on his knees in prayer that his knees became as calloused as those of a camel.

Time Line

James addresses his letter *to the twelve tribes who are scattered abroad,* which refers to the Jewish believers living outside of Palestine. These believers are besieged with problems that test their faith and lead to their dispersal. This concerns James as a leader of the church. He evidently feels the responsibility to exhort and encourage them in their struggles. This letter is believed to be one of the earliest writings of the New Testament because (1) it contains no mention of Gentile Christians; (2) it contains practically no distinctive theology; Christianity is viewed in terms of Messianic Judaism; (3) allusions to the teachings of Jesus have only slight agreement with the gospels; thus the letter probably preceded them; (4) the word *synagogue,* in addition to *church,* indicates a simple organization of elders and teachers; and (5) James does not mention the issues involved in the Council in Jerusalem in AD 50.

Time Line

6-5 BC	Birth of Jesus
5-4 BC	Wise men sought Jesus; Escape to Egypt
AD 6-7	As a boy Jesus visits the temple
AD 27-30	Jesus' public ministry
AD 30	Jesus crucified, raised, ascended, and Pentecost begun
AD 35	Stephen martyred, Paul's conversion
AD 44	James the disciple, son of Zebedee, beheaded by Herod Antipas
AD 45-49	James, half-brother of Jesus, wrote the Book of James
AD 46-48	Paul's First Missionary Journey
AD 50-52	Paul's Second Missionary Journey
AD 50	The Jerusalem Council met
AD 53-57	Paul's Third Missionary Journey
AD 58	Paul imprisoned and Acts ended
AD 62	James suffered a martyr's death
AD 70	Jerusalem destroyed by Rome

Note: The above time line was collectively prepared from the *Antiquities of Josephus; The Chronology of Biblical Christianity*; *The Open Bible* (Expanded Edition), New American Standard Version; and The Life Application Bible, New Living Translation.

Purpose of James

The purpose of the Book of James is to expose hypocritical practices and to teach right Christian behavior. James has been called the "Proverbs of the New Testament" because it is written in the moralistic style of wisdom literature. James, the person, is passionate in his preaching against inequity and social injustice. This has also earned him the title of "Amos of the New Testament."

Blueprint

This book could be outlined in several ways. *The Life Application Bible* suggests Genuine Religion, Genuine Faith, and Genuine Wisdom. *The New International Bible* suggests Greeting, Dealing with Tough Times, Listening and Doing, Favoritism Forbidden, Faith and Deeds, Taming Your Tongue, Two Kinds of Wisdom, and Warnings against Worldliness and Oppression. Other Bible references make further suggestions; however, for the purpose of this study we will use the following modified blueprint from *The Open Bible*.

> **1. The Tests of Faith:** These verses help us to develop the qualities of genuine faith regarding trials and temptations. Outward tests and inward temptations will be the focus of these verses.
>
> **2. The Characteristics of Faith:** These verses help us to know how we as believers are to respond to testing by developing the seven characteristics of faith. These characteristics include: obedience, impartiality, confirming actions, tongue control, wisdom, humility, and trust in God.
>
> **3. The Victories of Faith:** These verses encourage us to wait patiently for Jesus' return as we endure suffering, to be assured of God's purpose in our lives, to pray faithfully, and to confront and restore wandering believers.

Themes

As we already have discovered, James writes to persecuted Jewish believers who are scattered throughout the Roman world. In their new surroundings they evidently are tempted to let intellectual agreement pass for true faith. This book reminds us that true faith transforms lives. Thus, we are encouraged to put our faith into action. The major themes we will discuss are:

Faith
Endurance
Actions
Love
Obedience
Prayer
Trials
Wisdom

Overview Session Worksheet

Focal Passage: *This letter is from James, a slave of God and of the Lord Jesus Christ. It is written to Jewish Christians scattered among the nations* (James 1:1).

After you read the overview, please answer the following questions:

1. Four men named James are listed in the Bible. Which one do you believe wrote the Book of James? (Mt. 13:55; Mark 6:3)

a) James, the father of Judas (not Iscariot)
b) James, the half-brother of Jesus
c) James, the son of Zebedee
d) James, the son of Alphaeus

2. What evidence helped you determine which James is writing this book? (Acts 1:14-15; 15:13-29)

_____

_____

3. From Scripture we know that James does not always accept the claims of Jesus. What event took place that changes his heart and has a lasting impact on his life? (1 Cor. 15:7)

_____

4. Had you been a witness to the event in 1 Corinthians 15:7, what impact would this have had on your life?

_____

5. Traditionally, what type of person is James? (Acts 1:14; Gal. 2:9)

_____

6. James observes ____ _____ _____ as a testimony to other Jews (Acts 21:18-25). **Why?**

_____

7. According to Josephus, James suffers a _____ _____ death not long before the fall of Jerusalem.

8. The Book of James is one of the earliest writings of the New Testament. It is thought to have been written around AD 45-49. Before this book is written, what events are taking place that cause great concern for James?

_____

_____

_____

9. What is the purpose of the Book of James?

_____

_____

10. What is your purpose for studying the Book of James?

_____

_____

11. The Book of James is a letter written in the moralistic style of wisdom literature; therefore, it has been called the _____ ___ _____ _____

_____.

12. From the major themes throughout the Book of James, which one do you believe will help you grow closer in your relationship with your Heavenly Father and your commitment to our Lord Jesus?

_____

_____

Week 1
Tests of Faith

Day 1
When Troubles Arrive

Day 2
A Doubtful Mind

Day 3
Responding to Temptations

Day 4
Listen Twice, Speak Once

Day 5
Characteristics of Faith
Characteristic 1: Faith Obeys the Word

This week initiates our daily Bible study on the Book of James. We are in for some pretty heavy material even this first week, so make sure you are prayed up, have God's Word open, and are ready to proceed with some real introspection. As you see, chapter 1 covers a wide variety of topics; however, some topics will be discussed in more detail as we progress through the chapters. Just looking over the topics makes me either cringe or laugh, because I have "been there and done that." As believers we know that our Heavenly Father walks with us wherever we go. We have the assurance that as painful as some things might be, things always work out for our good. By the way, a sense of humor really helps to get us through most anything. Reckon I've rambled enough. So pour yourself a cup of coffee or tea, get into your favorite study chair, and let's begin. I am so happy that you are in this study with me as we explore His truths together.

<u>Heart Truths</u>
Day 1: James 1:2-3
Day 2: James 1:5-6a
Day 3: James 1:13
Day 4: James 1:19
Day 5: James 1:22

Week 1, Day 1

When Troubles Arrive

Today's Focus: James 1:2-4, 12; Matthew 8:25-27; 9:35-38; 1 Peter 1:6-7; 4:12-16; 5:10; Psalms 3:3-5; 56:3; 66:10-12

In our introductory session we established that James is the half-brother of Jesus and that this book is one of the earliest letters written, possibly even preceding the four gospels. We also know that after Stephen is martyred, persecution increases. It scatters the Jewish believers throughout the Roman world. Consequently, because these believers do not have the support of the established church, they are besieged with problems testing their faith; evidently they have succumbed to impatience, bitterness, materialism, disunity and spiritual apathy. *Hmmm*, sounds like today, doesn't it? Anyway, James, a prominent leader of the early church, feels the responsibility to warn as well as encourage these believers in their faith struggles. Wow! Don't we need the same warnings and encouragement today? I know I do!

James does not waste any time; immediately after his greeting in verse one, he delves into the topic of experiencing trials. The Greek word for trials is *peirasmos* (pronounced *pi-ras-mos*) and means adversity, troubles, experiences of evil, and putting to proof by experiment. I am interested in the fact that trials can be viewed as an experiment which actually is an assessment of who we are and how we hold up under the stress of troubles. *Hmmm*, does that mean trials build your character? Of course it does. Let's see what God's Word says.

♥ **Read Psalms 66:10-12. In reflecting back over some trials or troubles you have experienced, how did you feel when these were all over and you moved on? Describe below.**

_____

_____

According to the psalms when we experience trials, we are purified like silver melted in a crucible. Trials test our faith, build our character, and give us opportunity for growth. Maybe we should consider trials to be gifts from God, because after the experience we are better people. But sometimes when we go through trials, we feel really abandoned. In Scripture, so does King David. However, when

17

David feels abandoned, he tells God about it. What do you have in common with King David? How do you differ? Do you tell God what you really think and feel? Do you truly recognize Who listens to your prayers? If you open your heart and are totally honest with your Heavenly Father, your understanding of Him will grow.

♥ **Read Psalms 3:3-5. What assurance can you gain from these verses?**

_____

_____

David firmly believes God protects him when he sleeps and when he is awake. He has the assurance that when everything goes wrong, God is there for him. David knows God is his shield and that he can overcome all fears by trusting in God for protection. What about you? When you experience troubles, can you trust God for protection? Can you say, *What time I am afraid I will trust in thee* (Ps. 56:3 KJV)? If not, why not? Let's see what Jesus does.

♥ **Read Matthew 8:25-27. In these verses what do the disciples witness?**

_____

_____

Wow! Jesus even controls the forces of nature. Do you realize who Jesus really is? Do you comprehend Who God really is? Do you realize that He can control the storms you encounter in your life? Whether your storms are from nature or from the troubles you face, He has the power to control them. Jesus is willing to help, but first we must ask! That means we must pray first for His help. Hope and confidence in our Heavenly Father far outweigh our fears and troubles. Believe it or not, trials will make us stronger and prepare us for the future. What makes the difference? Do I really have to be joyful in my troubles?

♥ **Read James 1:2. When you read this verse, how did you respond?**

_____

_____

Note that James does not say *if* trials or troubles arise; instead he says *when* trials or troubles occur, let them be an opportunity for joy. Also, notice that he uses the plural and not the singular form for *troubles,* which is an indication that we will experience not just one trial but perhaps several as we walk through our lives. Now I have to admit, I did not always understand what being joyful when troubles arrive means. Through the years I have begun to realize that I do not have to pretend to be happy about facing pain. However, having a positive outlook when trials arrive is important. I truly can consider them opportunities for joy because of what can be produced in my life.

♥ **Compare James 1:2-4 with 1 Peter 1:6-7. As you read these verses, what major similarities and differences can you identify?**

_____

_____

_____

_____

Both James and Peter tell us that our faith will be tested and to consider this to be joy when that happens, as it will make us strong. However, James says it is for our endurance to have a chance to grow; this will make our character strong and ready for anything. The Greek word for _endurance_ is _hupomone_ (pronounced _hoop-om-on-ay_) and means cheerful waiting, patience, withstanding, and persevering. Peter says trials will make us strong and will purify us like gold; this will bring us praise, glory, and honor when Jesus returns. In the refining process of gold the impurities are burned away; this makes the gold beautiful and shiny. So whether they happen for endurance or purification, trials definitely will affect our lives.

As you know, we will face trials when we let our lights shine into the darkness. Thus we can accept troubles as part of the refining process that burns away our impurities and prepares us to meet Jesus. Trials teach us patience and help us grow into the kind of people God wants to use for His glory. However, we have a choice, don't we? We can turn tough times or trials into opportunities for learning perseverance that will help us grow into godly people, or we can grumble, criticize, and feel sorry for ourselves. Whatever our choice, we will have trials. If you think about it, they are a lot easier to deal with if we turn them over to our Heavenly Father and allow Him to walk with us through them. What is your choice?

♥ **Think of a situation in which you have been unpleasant and complained about your troubles. What was the result?**

_____

_____

♥ **Now think of a time when you have been joyful in your troubles? What was the result?**

_____

_____

♥ **Did you notice any difference in the way you responded in the above situations? What made your results different?**

_____

_____

19

Sometimes we do not know the depth of our character until we see how we react under pressure. Can we still be kind to people who mistreat us? What about people who are prejudiced against us or lie about us or treat us unjustly? I believe with all my heart that God wants to mature each of us. So instead of complaining about our struggles, let's see them as opportunities for growth. Let's thank Him for His promise to walk with us and carry us in His arms through the rough times. Let's ask Him to help solve our problems and to give us the strength to endure them. Then wait, be patient, and believe He will help.

♥ **Read James 1:12. What does God promise to do if people patiently endure testing?**

_____

_____

God promises not only to bless us but to give us the crown of life—our reward of eternal life. Wow! We will be there in heaven with the living God forever! Peter tells us not to be surprised at the trials we are going through. Instead, he says to be happy, because these trials make us partners with Jesus in His suffering. Just think, afterward we will have the joy of sharing His glory when it is displayed to the entire world. Peter further tells us to be happy when we are insulted for being Christians, as NO shame is involved in His name. He also tells us the Holy Spirit will come upon us (1 Pet. 4:12-16).

One of my favorite verses is 1 Peter 5:10, which reads, *And after you have suffered for a little while, the God of all grace, who called you to His eternal glory in Christ, will Himself perfect, confirm, strengthen, and establish you* (NAS). What do these four words mean?

♥ **Think about it: how would you define the words in the above verse?**

Perfect

_____

Confirm

_____

Strengthen

_____

Establish

_____

To me this verse is God's promise to us when we suffer trials or troubles. The God of all creation, our Heavenly Father, promises to restore us completely, to support us unconditionally, to give us His power, and to place us on a permanent foundation. Isn't that awesome? Keep in mind and be encouraged, because our greatest lessons in life emerge from the pain we experience. Why? Rick Warren has said that troubles make us focus more on God, build our character, draw us closer to others in fellowship, provide us with a ministry, and give us a testimony to share. But as believers, we have a greater responsibility.

♥ **Read Matthew 9:35-38. What does Jesus encounter in every place He goes?**

In the Bible, everywhere Jesus travels, He encounters people with problems so great they do not know where to go for help. Thus He tells His disciples He needs workers who will know how to deal with the problems of other people. That's you and me! Do you realize that every trial you endure will help you to comfort another person who is dealing with a similar problem? As believers we are commissioned to help others with their troubles, to comfort them, show them the way, encourage them, and give them hope.

When troubles arrive, how have you decided to react? A *faith that works* considers everything joy when trials are encountered, because we know the testing of our faith produces endurance. We may not be happy that a trial has occurred, but we certainly can be joyful in knowing that Jesus, through the Holy Spirit, will be with us through all of our trials and troubles. We have a choice. What's your choice? Let's count it all joy!

---♥---

Your Thoughts

Questions

Comments

Prayer Requests

Prayer Answers

Week 1, Day 2

A Doubtful Mind

Today's Focus: James 1:5-8; Mark 11:23-24; Genesis 3:1-6; Matthew 11:4-6; 14:28-31; 21:21-22

What does having a *doubtful mind* mean? The Greek word for *doubting* is *diakrino* (pronounced *dee-ak-ree-no*) and means to withdraw from, to hesitate, or to separate thoroughly. In today's language it may mean to be wishy-washy or to have a lack of faith. So what does *faith* mean? The Greek word for *faith* is *pistis* (pronounced pis'-tis) and means assurance, belief, persuasion, and/or system of religious truth. Obviously, these two words form a dichotomy and have opposite meanings. With these definitions in mind, let's see what James says to the scattered Jewish believers.

♥ **Read James 1:5-8. After reading these verses, can you relate to the analogy used to describe a doubtful mind? Please give an example.**

_____

_____

In verse six James uses the analogy that a doubtful mind is as unsettled as the waves of the sea that are driven and tossed about by the wind. Can you picture that? Close your eyes for a moment; try to picture yourself standing in the water on a beach, with waves from the sea splashing against your body. How are you feeling? Are you rocking to and fro from the force? Are you losing your balance? Are you feeling any apprehension? What do the waves look like? Are they gigantic or small in nature? Well, if you have as vivid of an imagination as I do, I'm not getting into that water if the waves are really big. In fact, I prefer to stand on the shore and watch instead of being in the middle of them. Ouch! If we are believers, are we supposed to watch from a distance and not get our feet wet? *Hmmm,* is that what a doubtful mind is like?

A doubtful mind is not completely convinced that God's way is the best way. This type of mind treats God's Word as though it is any ordinary piece of advice. Instead of obeying all of God's Word, this type of mind retains the option to disobey if it doesn't agree. It vacillates between following God's way and the desires of one's own heart. Doubt has left this person as unsettled as the waves of the sea.

James says this type of person should not expect to receive anything from the Lord, because such a person wavers back and forth in everything he or she does. Who or what causes doubt?

♥ **Read Genesis 3:1-6. Who or what causes Eve's doubt?**

_____

♥ **In what way can you relate to Eve?**

_____

From these verses we know Satan is the one who causes Eve to have doubts about God's goodness. He makes Eve forget all that God has given her; instead, he makes her focus on the one thing she is not supposed to have. Isn't that how we also get into trouble? Rather than counting God's blessings we focus on what we do not have. Read further.

♥ **Read Matthew 11:4-6. How does Jesus deal with John's doubt?**

_____

_____

As John sits in prison, doubts begin to plague him as to whether Jesus really is the Messiah. Jesus answers John's doubts by pointing to the evidence: His miracles, healings, and preaching. Sometimes we can see and understand only from our own human perspective rather than from God's perspective. If our doubts lead to questions and those questions lead to answers, then doubt has done some good. Questioning can help sort out our beliefs and strengthen our faith. However, questioning can make us vulnerable, as doubt can cause us to sin, which harms faith. Satan knows that once we begin to question, he more easily can make us do what he wants. Actually we can let doubt deepen our faith or divide it. But, be careful, as a divided mind only causes problems. We cannot be self-centered and God-centered at the same time.

♥ **Read Mark 11:23-24. What two things are required if we have faith?**

_____   _____

Several times in Scripture we hear Jesus say, *"O you of little faith."* Those words make me feel sad, because we know that all things are possible with God. If we have the faith He requires of us, then we must really believe and not doubt in our hearts. He says we can pray for anything, and if we believe, we will have it. I could go on and on about prayer, but James covers it at length during our last week of study. Just know prayer is truly one of my favorite topics; my life is a testimony to the power of prayer.

Many times you probably have read the story of Jesus walking on the water, but let's focus for a minute on Peter (Mt. 14:22-33). Remember Peter's reaction when he sees Jesus approach him? Let's discuss what happens.

♥ **Read Matthew 14:28-31 and answer the following questions.**

What does Peter desire to do?

_____

What happens to Peter when he is able to carry out his desire?

_____

What does Jesus say to Peter in this situation?

_____

Thinking about these verses, have you ever gotten "out of the boat" to take a step of faith? If so, explain.

_____

Bible scholars often criticize Peter and give him a tough time because he doubts. But Peter deserves credit for the fact that he is the only disciple who actually gets out of the boat. We can speculate as to why Peter wants to walk on the water in the first place. We also can see that when Peter allows fear to overcome him, he begins to sink. Jesus rebukes him for doubting Him. But on whom does Peter call when he begins to sink? And Who immediately reaches out and grabs him? Think about it!

How decisive are you? Do you rely on God? Do you totally trust Him? Or are you straddling the fence? Do your actions reflect your words? Are you letting doubt deepen your faith or destroy it? Are you depending on the Holy Spirit for guidance? Are you seeking mature Christian companions? Are you reading and studying God's Word? To have a *faith that works* and removes doubts, doing these things is necessary.

At one time or the other, we all will have doubts, especially if we focus on the waves that difficult circumstances produce around us. Then we, too, may sink. However, if we maintain our faith when situations are difficult and focus on the power of Jesus instead of our own inadequacies, we may soar like eagles. Jesus says, "*I assure you, if you have faith and don't doubt, you can do things like this and much more. You can even say to this mountain, 'May God lift you up and throw you into the sea,' and it will happen*" (Mt. 21:21). Wow! Go away doubt; I want faith! What about you?

--- ♥ ---

Through his devices of doubt, distrust, discouragement, and deception, Satan tries at every turn to prevent or steal your harvest and keep you from reaching greater fruitfulness.

Bruce Wilkinson

Your Thoughts

Questions

Comments

Prayer Requests

Prayer Answers

Week 1, Day 3

Responding to Temptation

Today's Focus: James 1:13-18; Proverbs 6:16-19; 2 Timothy 2:22; 1 Corinthians 6:9-11; 10:13; Matthew 4:1-11

Do you think *temptation* is the same as *being tested*? Let's take a closer look and see. According to the *Life Application Dictionary/Concordance, temptation* is an enticement to sin, whereas *tests* are trials intended to ascertain value, quality, or character; in other words, to examine. James says temptation originates from the lure of evil desire; in contrast, God blesses people who patiently endure testing. James also warns us that evil desires lead to evil actions; evil actions lead to death. Evil desires are from within us, NOT from God. Perhaps the desire may begin with an evil thought. If we dwell on it, it will become sin if we act on the desire. It is like an untreated cancer; it gets bigger and bigger until it finally destroys us.

♥ **Read Matthew 4:1-11. What is Jesus' reaction when Satan tempts Him in the wilderness?**

_____

_____

As believers, we often wonder why we still have temptations, but then we look at Jesus and see that the Scripture shows He is tempted by Satan. God doesn't tempt anyone; instead, he tests people. However, God allows Satan to tempt us to refine our faith and to help us grow more dependent on Jesus. Jesus can show us how to deal with this.

As you know from the Scripture, Jesus has been fasting for 40 days. Consequently, He is hungry, tired, alone, and weak, but He chooses not to use His divine power to satisfy His natural desire. Intellectually we know that God's Word is a sword to be used in spiritual combat. However, Jesus resists Satan by not only quoting Scripture but also by obeying it. That is our key. Knowing and obeying God's Word helps us follow God's desire rather than Satan's desire. Many of our desires are normal and good, but God wants us to satisfy them in the right way and at the right time.

Satan tempts us in the areas in which we are the most vulnerable, especially when we are under physical or emotional stress. However, he also tempts us through our strengths when we are most susceptible to pride. *Hmmm*, does that mean we must be on guard at all times against Satan's attacks? Absolutely! Many times we try to offer excuses or blame others for our evil thoughts and wrong actions.

♥ **Think for a moment. Name some of the excuses you make for your behavior.**

_____
_____
_____
_____

Let's see if you thought of some of the same excuses that I did. One of the first excuses that sprang to my mind was that "the devil made me do it." Years ago, Flip Wilson, a comedian, used that phrase over and over again during one of his monologues. Another excuse I heard especially from my children was "everybody's doing it.' Now, being the stubborn person that I am, that one did not hold water with me. When they tried to use it, I either ignored them or made them name "everybody" who was doing it. Other excuses you may have thought about are: "it's not my fault; it's the other person's fault," "I could not help it," "it was only a mistake," "nobody's perfect," "I was pressured into it," "I didn't know it was wrong," and even, "God is tempting me", which from the Book of James we know is not possible. Did I imagine some smiles on your faces as these excuses were named? If so, then maybe you are as guilty as I have been. People who make excuses for their behavior are just trying to shift the blame from themselves to either God or to someone else. As believers we are taught that we are to accept responsibility for our wrongs, confess them, and ask God for forgiveness. When you are tempted, consider whether Satan is trying to block God's purpose for your life like he tried to do with Jesus. We can turn to our Lord for strength. Read on.

♥ **Read 1 Corinthians 6:9-11. From these verses what are some sins for believers to avoid?**

_____
_____

In our permissive society sometimes we as believers overlook or even tolerate immoral behavior such as drunkenness, yet we become outraged at other immoral behavior such as thievery. According to God's Word we cannot be selective about what we condemn or excuse. God expects those who follow Him to have and maintain high standards.

♥ **Read Proverbs 6:16-19. Name the seven things the Lord hates.**

_____

_____

_____

♥ **Can you identify with any of these seven things? Name one that has present-ed a problem for you either now or in the past. Please explain.**

_____

_____

Temptation can take many forms. Do any of these seven things apply to you as they have applied to me? Notice that the only overt act is murder; the others we do with our tongues, our feet, and even our desires. Ouch! Now I suppose we have groveled on the ground enough. Since I am feeling as low as a snake, let's see how we can overcome these temptations. Turn in your Bible and read 1 Corinthians 10:13 NAS: _No temptation has overtaken you but such as is common to man; and God is faithful, who will not allow you to be tempted beyond what you are able, but with the temptation will provide the way of escape also, that you may be able to endure it._ Hallelujah! _Whew!_

To me this verse is such an encouragement. First of all, I feel relieved to know that others experience the same temptations that I do and that I am not alone in this struggle; neither are you. Second, God is so faithful! He keeps temptations from overpowering us and even provides us with a way out. Praise the Lord! Third, God helps us resist temptation by helping us to recognize people and situations that give us trouble. Fourth, He encourages us to RUN from anything we know is wrong, to choose right over wrong, to pray for God's help, and to seek godly friends who can help us when we are tempted. Remember: running from a tempting situation is the first step on the way to victory (2 Tim. 2:22).

Therefore, we understand that a difference really exists between being tested by God and being tempted to do evil by Satan. God is holy and sovereign and will not tempt anyone to do wrong. However, we know God allows Satan to tempt people to do evil. But we also know that what Satan intends for evil, God intends for good. Therefore, the best time to stop a temptation is before it is too strong or moves too fast to control.

The Bible says to RUN from evil, resist the devil, and he will flee from you. To have a _faith that works_ I must have my running shoes on. What about you?

-- ♥ --

Thorns do not prick you unless you lean against them, and not one touches without His knowledge.

Mrs. Charles E. Cowman

Every good gift and every perfect gift is from above
(Jas. 1:17a NKJ).

Your Thoughts

Questions

Comments

Prayer Requests

Prayer Answers

Week 1, Day 4

Listen Twice, Speak Once

> **† Heart Truths:**
>
> *. . . let everyone be quick to hear, slow to speak and slow to anger . . .*
> (Jas. 1:19 NAS).

Today's Focus: James 1:19-21; Proverbs 10:19; 15:1; Psalms 119:11; Ecclesiastes 5:2-3; Ephesians 4:26-27; Hebrews 2:1; Revelation 2:7; Matthew 12:34-37; 1 Kings 19:11-13

Someone has said that God gave us two ears and one mouth; therefore, listening is twice as important as speaking is. I do not believe that this is coincidental: the word *listen* is mentioned 470 times in God's Word, as compared to the word *speak* that is mentioned half as much at 222 times. Over and over again, God says, *Anyone who is willing to hear should listen* (Rev. 2:7). So what does *to hear* and *to listen* mean? Does a difference exist? Let's take a closer look and see.

According to the *Life Application Dictionary/Concordance*, *to hear* means to perceive sound and to heed what is being said; *to listen* means to absorb and accept information about God or someone else. Many times in my married life my precious husband has said to me, "Honey, you hear me, but are you really listening?" *Hmmm*, maybe I had better explain . . ..

Sometimes when my husband talks with me, my mind wanders off; I might not pay attention and consequently not listen to him as I should. Oh, I knew how to say the right words at the right time and how to pretend I was listening, but in reality I was thinking about something else or maybe even what I might say next. Well, having been caught, I had to take a long, tough look at myself and make a conscious decision to really begin to listen. The "funny" thing about this is that I expect him and others to give me their total attention. Don't you?

♥ **Read 1 Kings 19:11-13. Think about a time in your life when God may have revealed Himself to you in the same manner as He does Elijah in the Scripture. Did you hear Him?**

_____

_____

_____

♥ **What did you do about it?**

_____

_____

If we are not in the habit of truly listening when someone speaks, we may miss the gentle whisper of our Lord's voice, as it may occur when we least expect it. Many times God is found in the quietness of a humbled heart and not just in churches, conferences, and Bible studies. You are told to approach God with your ears wide open and to listen, for the life of your soul is at stake (Isa. 55:3). If we can't listen to each other, how can we hear God speak?

♥ **Read Hebrews 2:1. In this verse what are we admonished to do?**

_____

_____

♥ **Why do you think we are given this warning?**

_____

_____

Paying careful attention is diligent work and involves the focusing of our mind, body, and senses completely on what is being said. Pay careful attention to God's Truths, because if you do not, you can drift away into false teachings. Being quick to listen to the truth you hear from God's Word. Obeying His truth is vital to our spiritual health and well-being.

Now that we understand the importance of being quick to listen, let's take a look at the other side of the coin and determine why being slow to speak is very important.

♥ **Read Proverbs 10:19. After you read this verse, what is your response?**

_____

♥ **Read Ecclesiastes 5:2-3. Why are we warned to let our words be few?**

_____

_____

According to Proverbs and Ecclesiastes someone who talks too much is called a _fool_. A fool is a blabbermouth; a blabbermouth fosters sin. Why do you think that is true? Could this have something to do with our words reflecting what is in our hearts? Look with me at what Jesus had to say about this.

♥ **Read Matthew 12:34-37. Think about these verses. Why does Jesus remind us about the words we speak?**

_____

♥ Do you believe you are responsible for every word that proceeds from your mouth? Explain.

_____

Jesus reminds us that good words spring from a good heart and that we are responsible for every idle word we speak. We either will be justified or condemned by our words. Ouch! We have heard that those who speak much hear less. Why do you think that may be true? Words are so powerful. They can encourage or destroy. We are instructed to be careful with our words and be slow to speak, but how can we do this?

♥ Read Psalm 119:11. If we hide His Word in our hearts, it will keep us from

_____ .

That's right; if we keep God's Word in our hearts, it will prevent sin in our lives. That is why memorizing Scripture is so important. God's Word is a vital guide to have for every word we speak as well as for everything we do.

James also warns us to be _slow to anger,_ because words can stir up angry emotions. This is why we are told, _A gentle answer turns away wrath, but harsh words stir up anger_ (Prov. 15:1). Many times people raise their voices when they are angry; in turn this triggers an angry response. However, watch what happens when we whisper. Being angry when a person is speaking quietly is difficult. Our entire focus changes when we are forced to listen more closely to a whisper.

♥ Read Ephesians 4:26-27. How do you deal with your anger?

_____

_____

♥ To whom does anger give control?

_____

Most of us know that anger can be highly destructive; that is why dealing with our answer properly is essential. If we speak too quickly and without thought, anger hurts and can destroy relationships. It can cause bitterness which destroys from within like a cancer does. Anger erupts when our egos are bruised. Selfish anger never helps anyone. Therefore, deal with your anger immediately, or it will give Satan a foothold and an opportunity to separate us.

If this applies to you and you are angry with someone, you have a choice: You can nurse it, curse it, and rehearse it over and over again and allow Satan to use it to make you and the other person miserable. Or you can seek out the other person, confess it, forgive it, leave it, and allow God to bless it. What is your choice? If you are angry with someone, please take it away from Satan and give it to God; don't let the sun go down on your anger.

♥ **If you have chosen to deal with some unresolved anger, please record it in the space below so it will serve as a reminder of how God is working in your life.**

_____

_____

_____

What awesome advice James gives us: to have a *faith that works*, be quick to listen, slow to speak, and slow to get angry. To gain spiritual understanding, not only listen with your ears but also with your heart and mind. Oh, that it would be so in my own life! What about you?

---♥ --

I have a very clear idea how miserable your future will be unless you deal with your anger . . . it is like carcinoma of the spirit.
Max Lucado

Your Thoughts

Questions

Comments

Prayer Requests

Prayer Answers

Week 1, Day 5

Characteristics of Faith
Characteristic 1: Faith Obeys the Word

> † **Heart Truths:**
>
> *But prove yourselves doers of the word, and not merely hearers who delude themselves* (Jas. 1:22 NAS).

Today's Focus: James 1:22-25; Luke 6:46-49; Psalms 119:2; Romans 2:13; 7:7-8; 8:2; John 8:31-32; 13:17; 1 Peter 2:16; Matthew 7:21-27; 12:7; 28:20; 1 Samuel 15:22

Our previous day concluded a four-day study of the tests of faith as we dug deeply into God's Word on how to have a righteous response to trials, doubts, temptations, and listening more than we speak. Today begins our study of the seven characteristics of faith. For the next six weeks we will dig even deeper into each of these characteristics to gain understanding on how to apply them to our lives. I'm always fascinated to observe the order in which our Heavenly Father arranges things. Take special note that the first characteristic of faith James addresses is obedience. We will discover that true hearing means more than mere listening; it means having an obedient response to God's Word.

♥ **Think about the word** *obedience*. **In your own words how would you explain it to someone?**

_____

♥ **Read 1 Samuel 15:22. What does this verse say that obedience is better than?**

_____

According to the *Life Application Dictionary/Concordance*, *obedience* means submission to authority, complying with orders, and/or fulfilling one's responsibility. Actually I think obedience goes much deeper than that. To me it is a matter of one's heart attitude. If this were not so, then why does God say at least 10 other times in His Word that *"obedience is far better than sacrifice"*? Could He simply not want a hollow ritual? We can do all the right things: we can go to church, serve on committees, give to charity, pray, serve others, and read our Bibles, BUT if we do not do these out of love and obedience to God, they are just empty rituals. Our heart attitude toward God must occur first. Then and only then can we properly obey and observe religious rituals. Maybe that is why James uses the illustration of the mirror.

34

♥ **Read James 1:22-25. After you read these verses, what do you think God's mirror is reflecting in your own life?**

_____

_____

♥ **What do you see when you look into the mirror? Do you quickly glance at your reflection and then go on about your business, or do you study your appearance and see if you need to improve on it?**

_____

_____

How foolish you would be to look into a mirror after you eat a large meal and, having seen something between your teeth, ignore it and go on without trying to remove it! We are just as foolish to look into God's mirror of our lives and do nothing about the inner flaws He reveals to us that need correction. God's Word provides a unique mirror that shows our inner natures. Therefore, when He points out something in us that needs to be fixed, we had better listen and obey! _Hmmm,_ I wonder if that is also how we relate to God's Word. Do we only glance at it and go on about our business without allowing it to affect our lives? OR, do we take an intentional, deep look and allow His Word to show our flaws and make an effort to change? What about you? How does God's mirror influence you?

♥ **Read and compare Luke 6:46-49 with Matthew 7:21-27. What are the two types of people in these stories?**

_____

♥ **In what way can obedience be a strong foundation in your life?**

_____

How strong is your foundation? Luke and Matthew discuss the foolishness of disobedience and the importance of practicing obedience to weather the storms of life. Building on solid rock means not only to listen but to respond in obedience. Many people are headed for destruction because of their stubbornness or thoughtlessness or irresponsibility. Part of our jobs as believers is to help others stop and think about where they are headed. If they are building on the sand, we can help them realize what their consequences will be. Sometimes that waterfront lot is not what it seems to be! Beware that only sand is underneath the outward beauty. Does building on a strong foundation mean we can do anything we want? Let's take a closer look.

♥ **Read 1 Peter 2:16, Romans 7:7-8, and Romans 8:2. Does being *free* mean that you can do anything you want? Explain.**

_____

_____

♥ **Describe what being *free to obey* means to you.**

_____

_____

We may be free from keeping the law as a way to earn our salvation; however, we are only free to the extent we are willing to obey our Heavenly Father. That obedience must spring from the gratitude of our hearts for the FREE salvation Jesus gives us. Again, this goes back to our heart attitudes. We are free to live for God, not to do evil. Romans tell us the law shows us our sin and true freedom springs through the power of the Holy Spirit and through our Lord Jesus. John says that only in obeying God can true freedom be found (John 8:31-32). The law calls us to love God unconditionally and to love others as we would ourselves. But that's not all.

Paul tells us that not just knowing the law brings God's approval; obeying the law is what counts. Obedience brings blessings from our Heavenly Father (Rom. 2:13). We are not condemned for what we don't know but for what we do with what we do know. Jesus says we are held accountable by God and must do what we know to do. We are to obey with all of our hearts. So how do we do that? Even though our choice is to obey, only God can give us the power to obey Him with all of our hearts. Every time I obey, I have God on my side. My obedience is met instantly with His grace. David says, *Happy are those who obey his decrees and search for him with all their hearts* (Ps. 119:2). But we still need to consider still one more thing: we have a responsibility. Let's see what that is.

♥ **Read Matthew 28:20. What is your responsibility toward new disciples?**

_____

That's right! Just as we are to obey, our responsibility as believers is to teach others to obey all of God's commands. By obeying God, we begin to understand the very nature of God. The same responsibility exists with those of us who have children. When our children obey us, only then do they understand who we really are and that we want only what is best for them. Are you willing to have an obedient response to God's Word? Are you willing to teach others to obey? If your heartfelt desire is to have a *faith that works*, then obey God's Word and put His truths into practice. That's how faith works!

The golden rule for understanding spiritually is not intellect, but obedience.

Oswald Chambers

Your Thoughts

Questions

Comments

Prayer Requests

Prayer Answers

Week 2
Characteristic 2:
Faith Removes Partiality

Day 1
Showing Favoritism

Day 2
Removing Discrimination

Day 3
Loving Your Neighbor

Day 4
Judging by the Law of Love

Day 5
Being Merciful

This second week of Bible study spotlights the first 13 verses of chapter 2 in the Book of James. The focal point of these verses is the *Second Characteristic of Faith: Faith Removes Partiality.* So get comfortable physically, because you may not be so comfortable spiritually or emotionally as we take a long, tough look at avoiding partiality in our lives. Not exactly my favorite subject; however, it is very dear to my heart. You might even say I have become an advocate for fair treatment. Why? Because many different forms of partiality exist. At one time or another I have been the target of prejudicial treatment. This may even have happened to you, too. As some of you may know, partiality hurts and hurts deeply. By any other name partiality can be called *rejection;* no one likes to feel rejected. Let's continue to lift each other up in prayer as we see what truths our Heavenly Father wants to teach us about removing partiality. I am so pleased that you have made it with me to this second week. Let's begin.

Heart Truths
Day 1: James 2:1
Day 2: James 2:4
Day 3: James 2:8
Day 4: James 2:12
Day 5: James 2:13

Week 2, Day 1

Showing Favoritism

Today's Focus: James 2:1-4; 3:17; Genesis 37:3-4; Malachi 2:9; Acts 10:34; Deuteronomy 10:17

In our previous week together, our minds were broadened as we examined the *tests of faith*. For us to have a *faith that works*, we discovered the biblical way to react when troubles occur—to replace doubt with faith, to run when Satan tempts us to do evil, to be quick to listen, to be slow to speak, and to be slow to get angry. The week concluded with a study of the *First Characteristic of Faith: Faith Obeys the Word*. We learned that not only are we to obey ALL of God's Word, but as believers we are responsible to teach others to obey His Word, thereby increasing our understanding of Who God really is.

This week we will focus on removing partiality. The Greek word for *partiality* is *prosopolepsia*, pronounced *pros-o-pol-ape-see' ah*. It means favoritism. So we will begin our first day's study by examining what happens when favoritism is shown and what it does to the persons involved—both the receiver and the giver, as well as the effects it has on others. Let's begin by asking ourselves a question:

♥ **Do you think showing favoritism is wrong?** _____ **Below explain your answer.**

_____

_____

Now that you have had a chance to reflect whether you think favoritism is wrong, let's see what God's Word says.

♥ **Read Genesis 37:3-4. After you have read these verses, explain why you think showing favoritism is dangerous.**

_____

_____

Most of you are familiar with the story of Joseph's brothers selling him into slavery. Have you given much thought as to why his brothers act this way toward him? Scripture does not beat around the bush. It says Jacob loves Joseph more than he does any of his other children because Joseph is born to him in his old age by the "love of his life"—Rachel. One day Jacob gives Joseph a special gift of a beautiful robe—not just any robe but a robe suitable for royalty. The Bible further says that his brothers hate Joseph because of their father's partiality and that they cannot even say a kind word to him. OUCH!

What do we learn from this story? Jacob favors Joseph; the beautiful robe becomes a symbol of that favoritism. This really aggravates his brothers. Perhaps they have feelings of anger, bitterness, jealousy, resentment, and hurtfulness which cause a division in the family. *Hmmm*, does this behavior and do these feelings sound familiar in today's world? You know the rest of the story after Joseph is sold into slavery by his brothers, so we will not elaborate further. However, we also see a parent who outwardly displays favoritism toward one of his children and is filled with grief when he thinks Joseph is dead. Parents may not be able to change the way they feel toward a child, but they surely can change their actions, especially toward the other children. Because of Jacob's overwhelming partiality, we see the effects that favoritism has on the giver, the receiver, and the others involved.

I can remember the hurtful words of my mother as she recounted the partiality that my grandmother bestowed on my mother's brother. My mother always believed she was unloved; she had much anger and heartache that I believe she never got over. How sad for anyone to go to his or her grave with unresolved bitterness! Having experienced the reality of that situation is one reason I bend over backward, even today, to be fair to my children.

♥ **Read Malachi 2:9. After you read this verse, describe your reaction to what God does to the priests in the story.**

_____

_____

God's Word says that the priests show favoritism to people of influence and allow them to break the law. Evidently they have a double-standard based on wealth and/or social position. Our Heavenly Father does NOT play favorites! In fact, favoritism is contemptible in His sight. Therefore, because the priests are not obeying God and are showing partiality in their interpretation of the law, God makes them despised and humiliated in the eyes of the people. Sounds as though our Heavenly Father considers partiality a sin, right?

♥ **Read James 2:1-4 and 3:17, Acts 10:34, and Deuteronomy 10:17. What do these verses emphasize about partiality?**

_____

_____

James actually condemns acts of favoritism and stresses that God views all people as equals. He further states that God's wisdom shows no partiality. Because of the Jewish-Gentile conflict in Acts, Peter declares that God doesn't show partiality and that the message of Jesus is for everyone regardless of language, culture, prejudice, geography, economic level, or educational level (Acts 10:34). Even Moses distinguishes God as the One True God and emphasizes that God shows no partiality (Deut. 10:17).

What about motives? Could favoritism be a result of your inner motives? Are your motives pure or selfish? Do you love all people whether they are rich or poor? Do you focus on race, social status, sex, preconceived ideas, or personality differences? Do you have a sense of false pride when you deal with people? Do you stereotype people? What are your prejudices? Are they based on outward appearances, or do you look at the inward qualities of a person? Do you have a black or white, Jew or Gentile, Christian or Muslim conflict? In reality, where do you really stand with all of this? Think about how you would answer these questions.

From God's Word we have already discovered that favoritism is wrong. It affects everyone that is involved and is not an isolated situation. We have seen that favoritism is inconsistent with Jesus' teachings and results from evil thoughts. Favoritism insults people and is a byproduct of selfish motives. It goes against God's definition of *love*, shows a lack of mercy on the people involved, is hypocritical (demonstrates a double-standard), and quite frankly is a sin.

♥ **Looking back at the first question that I asked in our study today, has your answer changed as to why you think favoritism is wrong? If so, how?**

_____

_____

_____

To have a *faith that works*, remove partiality from your life. Do you have favoritism or partiality in your life? Chin up! Tomorrow we will study about how to avoid and remove discrimination that results from partiality. Praise the Lord (PTL), a way to remove partiality exists!

--♥ --

Dear Precious Father,
teach me to be fair in all my relationships and in all the areas of my life. Forgive me of my prejudices. Cleanse me of any favoritism that I may be inclined to show toward anyone. Harness my thoughts and purify my motives. Thank You for sending Jesus to be my role model, my Savior, and my Lord. Thank You for the power of your Holy Spirit, because I am helpless without Him. Mold me into the person You want me to be. I do desire to have a faith that works!
In Jesus' Name I pray, Amen.

Your Thoughts

Questions

Comments

Prayer Requests

Prayer Answers

Week 2, Day 2

Removing Discrimination

† Heart Truths:

. . . doesn't this discrimination show that you are guided by wrong motives? (Jas. 2:4).

Today's Focus: James 2:1-4; Isaiah 56:1-2; Proverbs 24:23; 1 Samuel 16:1-13; Matthew 10:2-4; Galatians 3:26-28; Genesis 5:3-5; Hebrews 12:2

Yesterday we studied about what happens when someone shows favoritism toward another person and how that affects everyone involved. We also understood from God's Word that our Heavenly Father does <u>not</u> show any partiality and treats everyone equally. Today we will take a serious look at our motives and see how to avoid and remove discrimination that results from showing partiality. I believe this is all a matter of our attitude and our choices.

According to the *Biblical Cyclopedic Index, discrimination* means making distinctions and is forbidden on the basis of wealth (Jas. 2:1-9) and personal righteousness (Rom. 3:10, 23). In the stories of Jacob and Esau (Gen. 27), Rachel and Leah (Gen. 29), and Joseph's family (Gen. 37) favoritism causes family friction and jealousy. I'm interested in the fact that favoritism and discrimination are forbidden in God's Word for parents, judges, and ministers. So if we do not fall into one of these three categories, does that mean we can show discrimination and/or favoritism? Absolutely not! I have to believe that our Heavenly Father does not want any of us to show discrimination or favoritism toward anyone. With this in mind how do we avoid and remove discrimination and favoritism? Let's look at what God's Word says.

♥ Read Isaiah 56:1-2. What are some ways you can demonstrate fair treatment to everyone?

_____

_____

♥ What will the Lord do if you are careful to treat everyone fairly?

_____

_____

The first way we are to avoid and remove discrimination is by demonstrating fair treatment to everyone. Isaiah says to receive God's blessings, be just and fair to all people, and do what is right and good. This is God's standard! God Himself is the standard of fairness. Whatever He does is fair, whether we understand it or not, because it is done by His power according to His moral righteousness. Thus our response is to go directly to Him in prayer and to follow the example of our Lord Jesus.

♥ **Read 1 Samuel 16:1-13. When you read about the warning the Lord issues to Samuel, how did you respond?**

_____

_____

The second way we are to avoid and remove discrimination is by being careful not to judge by outward appearance alone. When Samuel goes to anoint David, God warns him not to judge by outward appearance only. The Lord does not make decisions the way we do; instead He looks at the person's thoughts and intentions. I think of the words in the song that says, "While others see a shepherd boy, God may see a King." When people judge only by outward appearance, they may overlook that special person who would be the best one for the job at hand. As you know, physical appearance does not always reveal what a person is really like or what his or her true value is. We may not be able to see a person's thoughts and intentions; however, through prayer we can ask our Father to help us recognize the inner qualities of people. Perhaps this would be true discernment.

How many hours do we spend in front of a mirror each week maintaining and trying to improve the outward appearance? Wonder how much more time we should spend developing our inner characters. What about your heart attitude? Are you doing anything to improve it? I am so thankful that our Heavenly Father judges by faith and character and not by physical appearance.

♥ **Read Matthew 10:2-4. What kind of people does Jesus call to be His disciples?**

_____

_____

The third way to avoid and remove discrimination is through the realization that God calls ordinary people to do extraordinary things. We see from the list of disciples that Jesus calls people from all walks of life. He calls common folks such as fishermen and tax collectors, whether they are educated or uneducated. However, today, people think only certain people are fit to follow Jesus. Our Father can and will use anyone regardless of his or her "significance." I am so thankful that I don't have to be able to sing like an angel or be like anyone else to follow my Lord. I am thankful that He uses all my inabilities along with whatever talents He gave me. My friend, the same is true of you and others! So if we feel small and useless, remember that our Heavenly Father uses ordinary folks such as us to do His extraordinary work. How exciting!

♥ **Read Galatians 3:26-28. If you are a believer, do you feel called to be** *a child of God?*

_____

_____

♥ **What does Paul tell us we are no longer?**

_____

_____

The fourth way to avoid and remove discrimination is to make an effort to seek out and value people who are not just like you. Paul tells us that through faith in Jesus we are all children of God and that we are to be united. We no are longer separate like slave or free, male or female, Jew or Gentile. We naturally feel comfortable toward those who are like us and feel awkward around those who are different from us. However, when we allow those differences to separate us, then we are disregarding God's Word.

One of the most rewarding experiences of my life was when I submitted to my husband's desire to purchase a motorcycle. I had previously said, "Over my dead body." As a nurse, I had taken care of my share of "dead" bikers in emergency rooms and surgical centers. But after 32 years of marriage I told the Lord that if that is what He wanted us to have, then let the motorcycle "fit" me, too. Well, guess what? It "fit"! My husband bought it; we joined a Christian motorcycle organization. For two years we had the opportunity to attend various rallies and witness those tough bikers know the same Jesus I knew. Sensing the unconditional acceptance and love that those precious bikers gave me was an awesome experience.

In turn God gave me such a love for those big, burly, bearded men and those half-naked, tough women that I actually felt more at home with them than I did at the nursing school. Now were they "like" me? Well, maybe in a lot of ways, because we both needed love and acceptance. But in reality, no, for I was in charge of a nursing school during that phase of my life. I really do not believe those in authority over me liked their nursing director riding a motorcycle. I challenge you to "step out of your box" and make a point to seek out and love people who are not "like" you. You will find that you perhaps have a lot in common and will experience some real God-given joy!

Last but certainly not least is the fifth way to avoid and remove discrimination, which is to realize that each person is a valuable, unique creation of God (Gen. 5:3-5). If we think of it, going back to Adam and Eve, all humans are related. We are all from a family that shares one flesh and blood. So when any prejudice or desire to discriminate enters your mind, remember that we are all one in God's sight.

♥ Read Hebrews 12:2. How do you avoid or remove discrimination or prejudice?

_____

_____

Hebrews tells you that to live effectively, fix your eyes on Jesus, on Whom your faith depends, from start to finish. In reality only Jesus can break down and remove discrimination or prejudice. But you can make a heart choice to allow Him to do so. If you truly want a *faith that works*, treat others fairly, avoid judging only by outer appearances, realize that God calls ordinary people, seek out and value people who are not like you, and know that each person is of value to our Heavenly Father. What about you? What is your heart attitude?

--♥--

The first thing that happens after we have realized our election to God in Jesus is the destruction of our prejudices.

Oswald Chambers

Your Thoughts:

Questions

Comments

Prayer Requests

Prayer Answers

Week 2, Day 3

Loving Your Neighbor

> **† Heart Truths:**
>
> *If you really keep the royal law . . . "Love your neighbor as yourself", you are doing right*
> (Jas. 2:8 NIV).

Today's Focus: James 2:8-9; Luke 6:35; 10:27-37; John 15:12; Matthew 5:40-42; 7:12; 10:42; 22:37-40; Romans 13:8; Leviticus 19:18; Deuteronomy 6:5

What does loving your neighbor really mean? Just who is your *neighbor*? If you are a believer, most of your Christian life you have heard about God's love as contrasted to the love of humanity. You are probably familiar with the "love chapter" found in the 13th chapter of 1 Corinthians; however, let's look deeper. What is this *royal law* that James says we MUST keep? How do we keep it? Let's look at God's Word.

♥ Read James 2:8-9. Why do you think James so emphatically tells you to *Love your neighbor as yourself*?

_____

_____

The Greek word for *love* is *agapao,* pronounced *ag ap ah' o,* and means "beloved". Many times our Heavenly Father uses the term *beloved* when He refers to believers throughout the Scriptures. According to the *Life Application Dictionary/ Concordance* the word *love* means the ultimate expression of God's loyalty, purity, and mercy extended toward His people. This kind of *love* is to be reflected in human relationships of brotherly concern, marital fidelity, and adoration of God. Let that definition sink in for a few minutes!

♥ Read Luke 10:27-37. After reading this parable, with what three principles about loving your neighbor can you identify?

_____

_____

In these verses Jesus is telling the "Parable of the Good Samaritan" in response to the religious expert's question about how to receive eternal life. We observe the man responding with a quotation from the "Law of Moses" which says, "'*You must love the Lord your God with all your heart, all your soul, all your strength, and all your mind.' And, 'Love your neighbor as yourself'*" (Luke 10:27-37; Deut. 6:5; Lev. 19:18). As you know, these verses form the <u>basis</u> of all the laws about how people are supposed to relate to each other. However, as Jesus instructs from the parable, we notice it is much deeper and wider than we may have thought. We can recognize from this parable three principles about loving our neighbor. First, it shows that even though we can justify a lack of love, one NEVER is right in doing so. Second, our neighbor is any person that is in need regardless of race, creed, or social background. Third, *love* means that we act to meet the person's need. You have no reason good enough to refuse to help someone!

♥ **Read John 15:12 and Matthew 22:37-40. How do we see Jesus reinforcing this truth?**

_____

_____

The "royal law" is the command of our Lord Jesus, the King of Kings, who told us to "*Love each other in the same way that I loved you.*" In Matthew Jesus reinforces this truth as He discusses the two greatest commandments of loving God with all your heart, soul, and mind and loving your neighbor as yourself. ALL the other commandments are based on these two. Jesus says if we truly love our Heavenly Father and our neighbor, we naturally will keep the commandments.

Think about it! Can you measure how much you love yourself? If you cannot, how can you love your neighbor as yourself? I have to be very honest with you: sometimes I don't even like myself, let alone love myself, especially when I am being critical or mean-spirited. That is when I have to get down on my knees, pray, and ask forgiveness from my Heavenly Father for my bad attitude and critical spirit. I know that when I do, He is faithful to forgive me and to cleanse me from all my unrighteousness. Then, when I am clean, I am free to really love others once again. Also, some people are just downright difficult to love. The only way I can love them is through Jesus. What about you?

Let's look at another phrase: Jesus says we must love each other as He loves us. Jesus died for us! Does that mean we have to die for someone to show our love? We may not have to die physically for someone, but we may need to die to ourselves. I just know that sometimes my stubbornness and selfishness get in the way. When I relinquish myself to Jesus, then wonderful things start to happen; that special ability to love He has given me just flows. We can practice sacrificial love in other ways: listening, encouraging, and helping others. It's called giving of our time sacrificially and not hoarding it to ourselves. Someone has said, "Give all the love you can, then try to give a little more." *Whew!*

♥ **Read Romans 13:8. How did you respond when you read that Paul refers to love for others as a *debt*?**

_____

♥ **What do you think about his words?**

_____

Paul says that we are to pay all our debts except the debt of love for others, because we can never finish paying that. I believe Paul refers to the debt that Jesus pays on the cross for us. Because of Jesus' willingness to die for me and for you, we are permanently in debt to Him for His sacrificial love that He pours out for us. Thus by loving others as He commanded we can only begin to repay that debt. Oh, what a Savior! Praise the Lord that He loves us so much!

♥ **Read Matthew 7:12. In your own words state the "Golden Rule".**

_____

_____

♥ **Read Matthew 10:42. Name some ways your love for others can be measured.**

_____

_____

Most of us are familiar with the "Golden Rule"—to treat all people as we want to be treated. But what does this mean? This is not just a bunch of words. The "Golden Rule" means that how much we love God is measured by how we love and treat others (Mt. 10:42). Our Heavenly Father notices every good deed we do! Demonstrate your love, even to your enemies (Mt. 5:40-42; Luke 6:35). Avoid favoring anyone. Love means action. It means taking the initiative to meet specific needs. Now, that is easy to do with folks we naturally love or that love us, but love means doing this even to folks who dislike us and hurt us. So, for faith to work, we are to love our neighbor as ourselves. That means any person our Father places in our paths! Sounds as though it is a command and not a choice. What do you think?

When I think of "loving your neighbor", I am reminded of the words of a song written and sung by Bill and Gloria Gaither.

We have this moment today to hold in our hands,
And to touch as it slips through our fingers like sand,
Yesterday's gone,
Tomorrow may never come,
But we have this moment today.

49

To have a *faith that works*, don't put off loving your neighbor as yourself.

---♥ ---

But now abide faith, hope, love, these three; but the greatest of these is LOVE.

(1 Cor. 13:13 NAS).

The whole being of any Christian is Faith and Love . . . Faith brings the man and/or woman to God; love brings God to the man and/or woman.

Martin Luther

Your Thoughts:

Questions

Comments

Prayer Requests

Prayer Answers

Week 2, Day 4

Judging by the Law of Love

Today's Focus: Today's Focus: James 2:10-12; 1:25; Matthew 22:37-40; Mark 12:29-31; John 13:17, 34-35; 21:15-17; Romans 13:8-10; Colossians 1:8

Yesterday we spent time together studying what "*love your neighbor*" really means. Once again we discovered that our Heavenly Father does not show partiality and that He expects us to love ALL people.

Today we will examine the "Law of Love" and the appropriate way to judge by that law. However, first of all let's get clear on what the "Law of Love" means.

♥ Read James 2:10-12. What response did you have when you read these verses and realized what happens to you when you break just one law?

_____

_____

James informs us that if we break even one of God's laws, we are just as guilty as is the person who has broken all of God's laws. In other words we can't decide to keep some of the laws and put aside other laws that perhaps we may not like. James advises us to remember that whenever we speak or whatever we do, we will be judged by the "Law of Love"—the law that sets us free. Now what exactly does that mean? Let's look further.

In the previous lesson we learned that *love* means the ultimate expression of God's loyalty, purity, and mercy extended toward His people and that love is to be reflected in our human relationships. According to the *Life Application Dictionary/Concordance*, *law* means a binding decree or a universal principle. Simply put, we need to obey the law. So if we put the two words together, we discover that the *Law of Love* means that in all human relationships love is to be binding and must be expressed to reflect God's loyalty, purity, and mercy. So with that definition in mind, do we have an appropriate way to judge by the Law of Love? *Judging* means that a sentence is passed or that someone is punished or condemned. Is that really our job?

Even though judges exist today as they did in Old Testament times, we know human judgment has many weaknesses. For example God's Word says judgment is often circumstantial (Josh. 22:10-34); is sometimes wrong (Gen. 39:10-20); is hasty and revengeful (1 Sam. 25:20-35); is full of conceit (Esth. 5:11-14); and is prejudiced (Luke 7:38-50). Often a judgment is based on opinion, circumstances, morals, and conscience rather than on God's Law of Love. Praise the Lord we are not judges who decide whether the law is right or wrong. God made the law; only He has the power to rightly judge it. Our main job is to obey it! That reflects back to our *First Characteristic of Faith: Faith Obeys the Word.* For you to read, memorize, and meditate on God's Word is always good, but that is not enough. Obey it, too!

♥ Read and compare Matthew 22:37-40 with Mark 12:29-31. Did you notice any differences or similarities? If so, describe them.

♥ What does Jesus say about God's Law of Love?

In these two Scripture references we learn that God's Law of Love is positive and can be condensed into two basic principles: Love God and Love Others. As we discussed in an earlier lesson, these two laws summarize ALL of God's laws. When we love God completely and love others as we love ourselves, then we have fulfilled the intent of all the other laws. On the other hand when we fail to love, we break God's Law of Love. Maybe we need to ask ourselves, do we build up others or tear them down? Do our thoughts, decisions, and actions reflect God's Law of Love? Do we pray and ask God to demonstrate His love through us and to show us how to react in any given situation? *Hmmm,* tough questions; read further.

Have you ever wanted to pick and choose which laws you wanted to keep and which laws you think you can overlook or ignore? Have you ever said, "Better to ask forgiveness than to ask permission"? That is NOT biblical! Why? Because it goes against a law; James reminds us if we break even one law, we are guilty and have sinned. We must obey all the laws. The only standard we are to measure ourselves against is God's Law of Love. If you break it, ask for forgiveness and renew your relationship with our Heavenly Father and perhaps even with others.

♥ Read Romans 13:8-10. According to these verses what does love do for others?

♥ What does loving others do for you?

Paul reminds us that love does no wrong to anyone and satisfies all of God's requirements. How awesome is that! Jesus does not leave loopholes in the Law of Love. When love demands it, believers are to go beyond religious, civil, and human legal requirements and be imitators of God's Law of Love.

James also tells us that the law *sets us free*. What does that mean? Can we do anything we want to do? Think again! God's law points out our sin and gives us the opportunity to ask for God's forgiveness. It is NOT a free ticket to do anything we want to do—especially something evil. As believers we are saved by God's grace. Salvation is what frees us from the control of sin. *Hooray!* Actually we are only free to obey God; that is the bottom line! Let's look a little further; you will see what I mean.

♥ Read John 21:15-17. Why do you think Jesus asks Peter three times if he loves Him?

When Jesus challenges Peter about his love, the first and second time Jesus uses the Greek word *agapao*, meaning <u>sacrificial love</u>. However, the third time Jesus uses the Greek word *phileo*, meaning affection or <u>brotherly love</u>. Each time Peter responds to Jesus with the Greek word *phileo*. Peter has to look deep into his true inner motives and feelings which reflect who he really is. Jesus does not settle for shallow answers; He wants us to have a genuine response that springs from our hearts. My dear friend, how would you answer that question? Do you really love Jesus? Are you His friend? Think about it.

♥ Read John 13:17, 34-35. In what ways do you receive His blessing?

Jesus says now that we know these things, we are to DO THEM. That is how we receive His blessings. Love is much more than warm, fuzzy feelings; it is a genuine attitude of the heart that manifests itself in action. With love we can have an impact that goes far beyond our own borders. As believers we have no excuse for not loving others (Col. 1:8). Loving others as Jesus loves is essential. This kind of love through the Holy Spirit brings unbelievers to Jesus and keeps believers strong and united in the hostile world in which we live. For a *faith that works* we are to be living examples of Jesus' love. Are you doing this?

-------------------------------------- ♥ --------------------------------------

God smiles when we love Him supremely
and obey Him wholeheartedly.

Rick Warren

Your Thoughts:

Questions

Comments

Prayer Requests

Prayer Answers

Week 2, Day 5

Being Merciful

Today's Focus: James 2:13; Luke 6:36; Ephesians 2:4-6; 4:32; Matthew 5:7; 6:14-15; 18:21-35; Titus 3:5; Hebrews 4:16; Jude 21-23; Romans 3:23

In trying to understand how to be merciful I had to resolve in my own mind the differences between *mercy* and *grace*. I looked in the *Biblical Cyclopedic Index* and discovered that *mercy* means forgiveness, compassion, and the withholding of deserved judgment or punishment for our sins. *Grace* means the free, unmerited favor of God toward sinful people. My husband, Archie, stated the difference quite well when he said, "God's grace brought Jesus here, whereas God's mercy sent Jesus to the cross." Now let's look at the meaning of this statement. Because our Heavenly Father desires to have an eternal relationship with us and to provide us with a way to live with Him forever, He sends Jesus here. That is grace. Because our Heavenly Father wants to provide a way out of eternal punishment for our sins, He sends His only Son, Jesus, to go to the cross for us so that we will be forgiven. That is mercy. Simply stated, grace is God's favor; mercy is God's gift of forgiveness. Grace is a source of forgiveness, salvation, and faith. As believers we are under His grace. Praise the Lord! Let's go a step further.

♥ **Read James 2:13. In this verse you read that this kind of mercy wins over judgment. In your own words what does that mean for you?**

_____

_____

According to James kind mercy wins over harsh judgment every time. As we have studied, only God's mercy can forgive our sins. However, when we withhold forgiveness or mercy from others, especially after we have received it, we prove we do not understand or appreciate God's mercy toward us. An example of that is the parable of the unforgiving debtor.

♥ **Read Matthew 18:21-35. According to this parable what is the second action of the king toward the evil servant?**

_____

_____

What should the evil servant do for his fellow servant?

_____

_____

Since your Heavenly Father has mercy on you and has forgiven ALL your sins, always forgive other people. Because our precious Lord Jesus has completely forgiven us, let this produce an attitude of forgiveness toward others. If we do not forgive, we are placing ourselves above God's Law of Love. Read further.

♥ **Read Matthew 6:14-15. How did you respond to the warning Jesus gives in these verses?**

_____

Jesus says that if you forgive those who sin against you, then your Heavenly Father will forgive you. But if you refuse to forgive others, your Father in Heaven will not forgive your sins. This means just what it says: if we refuse to forgive others, then God will refuse to forgive us. Quite frankly, who do we think we are when we refuse to forgive? What does that say to other people? Could we be saying that we are not all sinners in need of God's forgiveness? I hope not, because according to God's Word, that is a lie. God's Word says, . . . _ALL have sinned and come short of the glory of God_ (Rom. 3:23 KJV). What does this mean to you? Here's a personal example of what it means to me.

Until Jesus changed him, my dad was a very harsh man. He said and did things that hurt me deeply. However, when I realized that I must forgive him because my Heavenly Father's mercy forgave me (Eph. 4:32), I received an awesome release from my past and had immediate peace. I can rejoice that my dad is in heaven today with Jesus and that I will see him again. I am not saying that forgiveness is easy; actually it is quite a character builder. But I am saying that as believers we are required to have a spirit of forgiveness.

♥ **Have you experienced a time in your life when you forgave someone even though that person may not have deserved your forgiveness? _____ If so, what lessons did you learn from that experience?**

_____

_____

♥ **Read Matthew 5:7. What does Jesus say you will obtain if you are merciful?**

_____

_____

As you know, this is one of the beatitudes. The beatitudes serve as principles of life or standards of conduct for all believers. The beatitudes tell us that we will be blessed by our Heavenly Father if we possess the qualities that Jesus mentions. Thus we witness Jesus saying that God will bless and show mercy to those who are merciful. We are to be merciful as our Father is merciful (Luke 6:36). Is God your role model where mercy is concerned?

♥ **Read Titus 3:5 and Ephesians 2:4-6. According to these verses what do you have because of God's mercy?**

_____

Because of God's mercy and love, He gives us life when He raises Jesus from the dead. By God's special favor we receive salvation. He saves us not because of the good things we do but because of His mercy. He washes away our sin and gives us new life through the Holy Spirit. _Hooray!_ Now, this is mercy!

♥ **Can you obtain mercy through prayer?**

_____

♥ **Read Hebrews 4:16. What do you find at the throne of God?**

_____
_____

Of course we can find mercy through prayer. But not only do we find mercy at the throne of our Heavenly Father, we also find grace to help us when we need it. How awesome is that! God is so good; let's approach Him boldly. As we progress through James, prayer will be discussed in detail and will be the main focus in the last chapter. Just remember, Jesus is our high priest; God is our king, counselor, and friend. Talk to Him; He answers prayer!

♥ **Read Jude 21-23. After you read these verses, name some things you are going to do while you wait for the eternal life that our Lord Jesus in His mercy promises to give you.**

_____
_____

Jude says we are to live in such a way that God's love can bless us because we show mercy to others. Mercy is the reason for our hope; it is the attitude of believers as we wait for the eternal life that our Lord Jesus will give us. How is your attitude? For a _faith that works_ are you showing mercy to others?

In our study today we discovered that mercy is received in salvation through forgiveness, taught as a principle of life, practiced as a gift, evidenced by God's provision, obtained in prayer, and our reason for hope. Mercy is God's forgiveness and compassion all rolled up as one. We have a choice whether to be merciful. I know what my choice is. What is your choice?

-- ♥ --

His grace teaches that those who partake of his mercy must copy it in their conduct.

Matthew Henry

Your Thoughts

Questions

Comments

Prayer Requests

Prayer Answers

Week 3
Characteristic 3:
Faith Confirms Itself by Actions

Day 1
No Works . . . Dead Faith

Day 2
Showing Faith

Day 3
Willing Actions

Day 4
Abraham, Justified by Works

Day 5
Blessing and Cursing

This third week of study focuses on the last 13 verses of James, chapter 2. These verses clarify the *Third Characteristic of Faith: Faith Confirms Itself by Action.* Most of us know that *faith without works is dead,* but what does that really mean? Jim Cymbala, author of *Fresh Faith,* expressed this best, " . . . living for Christ is far more than just gritting your teeth and sitting on your hands" (p. 175). Think about the picture those words bring to your mind. Vivid, wouldn't you agree? So let's see what this means for us as believers. During the next five days we will take a deliberate look at what putting our faith into actions means. Now you may want to get comfortable physically, because spiritually the ride may be a bit bumpy! By the way, I really appreciate your traveling along with me. Riding over these bumps and sharing together is a lot more fun.

Heart Truths
Day 1: James 2:17
Day 2: James 2:18
Day 3: James 2:20
Day 4: James 2:24
Day 5: James 2:26

Week 3, Day 1

No Works, Dead Faith

Today's Focus: James 2:14-17; 1 John 3:17-18; Isaiah 58:7; Matthew 25:35-36; Galatians 5:6; Philippians 2:12

In week two James emphasizes that a *faith that works* is a faith that removes ALL partiality. Because our Heavenly Father is NOT partial, we are to remember that we, too, are not to show favoritism. We also discovered some practical ways to avoid and remove discrimination, to love our neighbor as ourselves, to love others as Jesus loves us, and to be merciful to everyone.

This week we will focus on putting actions, or "feet", to our faith. The study will center on how to show our faith, examine our willingness to do good works or deeds, and identify and apply principles from the examples of Abraham and Rahab. But first let's take a look at what happens when no works are related to our faith.

♥ **Read James 2:14-17. What was your reaction when you say that James says your faith is dead and useless if you do not show it by good deeds?**

_____

_____

According to James our faith is dead and useless unless we prove and show it by good deeds or works. James stresses that true faith changes our behavior as well as our thoughts. We know that salvation is not earned by good works, but our actions are what show that we are committed to our Heavenly Father and that our commitment is genuine. Faithful works and loving deeds are hallmarks of effective Christian living and are proofs of our faith in Jesus. But how do we "show" our good deeds without appearing to be self-righteous or proud?

Years ago when I was working in home-health nursing, I was responsible for a caseload of patients. If I wanted the patient to listen and heed my healthcare teaching, I quickly learned that I first had to meet the need the patient presented. For example one day I entered the home of a new mother who needed instructions on caring for her new infant. She was very busy folding diapers, preparing a meal, and trying to meet the needs of her new infant. So I helped her fold clothes. This precious new mother was very impressed that I had helped her with such a "menial" task. As a result she was extremely willing to take the time and listen to my health-care teaching. The same is true of meeting needs of people with whom we are in contact on a daily basis. To me, to overlook an immediate need does not truly show love to that person. It perhaps represents thinking only about our own agendas.

♥ Read 1 John 3:17-18. What happens when you do not show your actions?

_____

By our actions we show we truly love people and that we know we are living in the truth. Do your actions reflect that you really love other people? What about sharing your money, your time, or even your possessions? Are you willing to do that? Let's look further.

♥ Read Matthew 25:35-36 and Isaiah 58:7. What actions do Jesus and Isaiah say that you are to take?

_____

Our faith lacks sincerity if it does not reach out to others in need. These actions do not depend on our wealth or even our ability or intelligence; they are actions we freely give—small kindnesses that express our love. Such actions glorify our Heavenly Father and reflect our love for Him. Actually we have no excuse for neglecting those who have deep needs. Keep in mind how a small kindness can make your day and even encourage and build you up. The same is true as we respond to others around us.

♥ Read Galatians 5:6. Think about this verse. Name some ways that you can express your faith in love.

_____

Paul states that faith expresses itself in love. In reality that can be a self-check for us. By expressing our love to others through our actions, we can monitor our faith and thus perform a self-evaluation of our faith. Have you done a self-evaluation of your faith? If so, are you pleased with the results?

God's Word says we are to be careful to put into action God's saving work in our lives and to obey God with deep reverence and fear (Phil. 2:12). Now to me that sounds a lot like a command. In actuality our Heavenly Father expects us to put feet to our faith by our actions. If we identify ourselves as Christians, then our faith must produce good deeds. The small kindnesses and good deeds are what make our faith work! When Jesus said to _feed my sheep_, I don't believe He gives us a choice.

What do you think? For you to have a *faith that works*, challenge yourself to carry out a small kindness and/or a good deed for at least one person today.

---♥ ---

Little Children, let us not love with word or with tongue,
but in deed and truth

(1 John 3:18 NAS).

Your Thoughts

Questions

Comments

Prayer Requests

Prayer Answers

Week 3, Day 2

Showing Faith

Today's Focus: James 2:18; Romans 3:28; Revelation 14:13; Matthew 5:16; 7:16-20

Yesterday we discussed the importance of putting actions to our faith. Today we observe James having an argument with an imaginary person who evidently is trying to separate faith and works. However, James responds with a challenge when he exclaims that he cannot see faith if no good deeds are apparent, but he would show his faith by his good deeds (Jas. 2:18). To me, James simply says that faith cannot be separated from actions, because true faith always results in a changed life that produces good deeds. But what is meant by *true faith*? Let's examine what God's Word has to say.

♥ **Read Romans 3:28. How are you made right with God?**

_____

_____

In Romans we read that we are made right with our Heavenly Father through faith and not by obeying the law. We can do NOTHING to earn our salvation—not by any good deed. We receive salvation only through faith. But what does true faith really mean to you? Let's examine what you believe about true faith.

♥ **To you, what is *true faith*? Describe below.**

_____

_____

♥ **Why do you think God saves us only through faith?**

_____

_____

True faith eliminates our pride because it eliminates <u>our</u> effort. *True faith* also eliminates our self-praise and instead makes us realize that faith is all about what God has done for us. We all know that no person can totally measure up to God's standards or the law. Thus to have *true faith* we need our Heavenly Father's help. Last but definitely not least, *true faith* is having a relationship with our Heavenly Father.

That relationship is far more important than is any action for God that we can perform. However, a balance must exist between *true faith* and showing our actions. So what is it? How is that balance achieved?

♥ **Read Matthew 7:16-20. How do you identify true believers?**

_____

_____

According to these verses Jesus is teaching about the fruit that is seen in people's lives. He says a healthy tree produces good fruit and an unhealthy tree produces bad fruit. We are able to identify a tree or a person by the kind of fruit that is produced. In other words we are to beware of people whose words sound religious but their actions do not support their words. Maybe they are motivated by money or power and want to glorify themselves rather than our Father in Heaven. Does this mean we are to examine every believer to see what type of fruit he or she produces? Perhaps so, but let's be careful that we do not go on witchhunts and throw out everyone who is not perfect. Then no one would be left, because none of us is perfect!

In her book, *8 Choices That Will Change a Woman's Life*, Jill Briscoe asks a pertinent question, "Am I practicing what I preach and preaching what I practice, so that unbelievers can see a little of this Spirit-filled philosophy worked out in me?" (p. 154). Maybe we need to ask ourselves the same question. What is your answer? So, where is the balance in all of this? Let's look further.

♥ **Read Matthew 5:16. In this verse what instructions does Jesus give believers?**

_____

_____

♥ **How do these instructions apply to you?**

_____

Jesus instructs us to let our good deeds shine for all to see, so that everyone will praise our Heavenly Father. To be of value to our Heavenly Father we as believers can influence the world around us. If we live for Jesus, we will be like lights that are shining for all to see. However, sometimes for one reason or the other we refuse to shine. Let's think how that can happen.

♥ **What are some ways you can hide your light? Describe.**

_____

_____

I wonder whether you thought of some of the same ways of hiding your light that I did. Here are some thoughts you may want to "try on for size".

1. We can hide our lights by being silent when speaking up is the better choice. Someone has said that silence often is mistaken for agreement. Ouch!

2. We can go along with the crowd. My children used to say, "But, Mama, everyone is doing it!" In reality, no such thing exists as EVERYONE doing anything.

3. We can deny that the light even exists. *Ugh!* Does that remind you of Peter, or someone else, or even yourself?

4. We can allow sin to dim our lights. My, now that one hurts! But you know that sin breaks the relationship with our Heavenly Father, so the warning is to stay confessed up and to run from sin!

5. We can refuse to explain our light to others. Sometimes we ignore those "divine appointments" that He sends our way. Oh, Father, forgive me!

6. We can ignore the needs of others. What about the beggar or the neighbor or the friend who cries out for our help? Are we there for them? If so, do we do this in a nonjudgmental way? I am so glad I cannot read other people's minds. Aren't you? Only our Father has that capability! Praise the Lord!

7. We can hide away and close the door of our hearts and our homes. Sometimes we literally refuse to be with others and retreat by watching TV or a video or by using the computer. This not only hurts our relationship with others, it also hurts our relationship with our Heavenly Father, which ultimately hurts ourselves. Ouch!

As Jesus says, we are to be beacons of light for others to see and in so doing make sure we give all the praise to our Heavenly Father.

Herein lies the balance. We see that faith and works cannot be separated without ceasing to be alive. In Revelation 14:13 John hears a voice from heaven saying, *"Blessed are those who die in the Lord from now on . . . for their good deeds follow them!"* Just think! The good deeds that you produce will last forever. Wow! That is a promise from our Heavenly Father. Nothing is done in vain.

A faith that does not move a believer to action is a faith that has a very feeble hold on what that believer claims to have. If your faith is not rooted in Jesus our Lord, it is worthless. As James states things, *I will show you my faith through my good deeds.* A faith that is seen in how we relate to others—now that is a *faith that works*! Remember, God's glory is what we want to shine through us. Let our actions glorify our Heavenly Father and not ourselves.

---♥ ---

Faith is like the hand that reaches up to receive what God has freely promised. If the devil can pull your hand back down to your side, then he has succeeded.

Jim Cymbala

Just as the body is dead without a spirit, so also faith is dead without good deeds

(Jas. 2:26).

Your Thoughts

Questions

Comments

Prayer Requests

Prayer Answers

Week 3, Day 3

Willing Actions

Today's Focus: James 2:19-20; John 6:38; Romans 12:2; Matthew 8:29; Hebrews 13:20-21; 1 Corinthians 15:58; Galatians 5:6

One of the central themes in the Book of James is that genuine faith always will produce good deeds. Consequently we have spent the past two days focusing on the importance of putting actions to our faith and showing our faith. Today we take an in-depth look at our actions as directly related to our willingness. In James 2:19-20 (NAS), we are told that even the demons know who God is and that they tremble. Then James asks a very pertinent question to see if we are *willing to recognize* that *faith without works is useless*. Let's see what he means.

What does being *willing* mean? *According to the Life Application Dictionary/ Concordance, willing(ness)* means that we have decision-making capacity, indicating a power of choice. Simply stated, being *willing* means we have made a choice to be eager, enthusiastic, ready, prepared, and/or agreeable. So, if that is the case, then are you *willing* to put your faith into actions? Let's see what God's Word has to say.

♥ **Read John 6:38. How did you respond to the reason Jesus gives for descending from heaven?**

_____

Jesus works in complete union with God the Father. He states that His purpose is to do the Father's will. As He walks on earth Jesus is *willing*! He is eager, enthusiastic, ready, prepared, and in agreement to do the Father's will of the Father. Aren't we also to have that same purpose? Let's look further into God's Word.

♥ **Read Romans 12:2. What are you willing to allow God to do to you?**

_____

_____

♥ **If you allow God to do this, then what will that enable you to do?**

_____

_____

God's Word says we are to allow our Heavenly Father to transform us into new people by changing the way we think. If we allow Him to do that, then we will know what He wants us to do; we will know how good and pleasing and perfect His will really is. Our Father has good and perfect plans for each of His children. He wants us to honor and obey Him. We can do that only if we allow Him to change the way we think. Now, if you have a stubborn streak as I do, then you may have to go through some real "character-building" times like I did to change the way you think. Only when we allow the Holy Spirit to renovate, re-direct, and re-educate our minds are we truly changed. I didn't say doing this was easy; it actually may be quite painful, but it sure is worth it! The secret is willingness. But, let's take an even further look.

♥ **Read Hebrews 13:20-21. In what ways does God equip you to do His will?**

_____

_____

From these verses we learn that our Father equips us with all we need for doing His will. He produces in us, through the power of Jesus Christ, all that is pleasing to Him. Our Heavenly Father changes us from within to give us the power to do His will to help others.

♥ **Read Matthew 8:29. How do the demons address Jesus?**

_____

The fact that James states that even the demons believe only one God exists and that they tremble is highly interesting to me. In Matthew, the demons identify Jesus as the Son of God, but they do not think they have to obey him. So what significance is that to us as believers? Believing is not enough. Faith is more than belief. Yes, by faith we accept Jesus as our personal Savior. Yes, we know He is the only one who can save us from our sin and forgive us. But we have to live out our faith by obedience to His commands. So could that have something to do with being _willing_ to put our faith into actions? What do you think?

♥ **Review Galatians 5:6. What are some ways you express your faith?**

_____

When we place our faith in Jesus, we express our faith in love for God and for others. When we are His children, loving others is as natural as breathing in and breathing out.

♥ Read 1 Corinthians 15:58. How do you, as a believer, respond to doing the Lord's work?

_____

_____

In Corinthians we are told to be strong and steady and always enthusiastic about the Lord's work, for we know that nothing we do for the Lord is ever useless. Nothing we do is useless. Sometimes we may become discouraged and even indifferent because we may not see results quickly enough. Don't get discouraged over what you perceive as a lack of results. Keep in mind His promise that no good deed is ever useless. What our Father begins, He finishes. However, for a *faith that works*, be *willing* to be obedient and do as He directs you. Remember: it's all about HIM.

-- ♥ --

We ought not to be weary of doing little things for the love of God, who regards not the greatness of the work, but the love with which it is performed.

Nicholas Herman

Your Thoughts

Questions

Comments

Prayer Requests

Prayer Answers

Week 3, Day 4

Abraham, Justified by Works

Today's Focus: James 2:21-24; Genesis 22:9-12, 16-18; 15:6; Romans 3:28; 4:20-21; Galatians 3:6-9, 24-29

We have been studying about faith and how it relates to our actions. Today we will take a look at Abraham and examine why God's Word says he is *justified by his works*. But first let's see what *justified* means and make sure we understand the difference in what Paul means by being *justified* and what James means.

♥ **Read James 2:24 and Romans 3:28. In your own words contrast what James and Paul mean by being *justified*.** (See Chart 2, The Two Perspectives of James and Paul, in the Appendix, page 219.)

_____

_____

James states we are *made right with God* when we are <u>justified</u> by works, whereas, Paul states we are made right with God through faith. Unlike what many scholars believe, these two statements DO NOT contradict themselves. I have lived long enough and read my Bible many times. I know in my heart as well as in my mind that God's Word NEVER contradicts itself. So what could these two statements really mean? First of all, we know that many words have several meanings and can be used in many different ways. Take the word *bear,* for example. We can *bear* a burden, or we can hunt a *bear*. The words are spelled the same way but used entirely different. So could the word *justified* possibly also be used differently or even be directed at two different things? As we compare, look at the chart on page 219.

From the chart we can see that James and Paul actually complement each other's writings rather than contradict each other, because they use the word *justified* from two different perspectives. We know that people receive salvation only by faith, not by anything they can do. We also know that saved people will express their faith by doing good deeds out of obedience. Simply stated, the proof of faith is in the doing! Aren't you glad that our Heavenly Father made our salvation so simple and not complicated? I sure am! Now let's see how Abraham is *justified* by his works.

♥ **Read James 2:21-24 and Genesis 22:9-12. Why do you think Abraham is declared right with God?**_____

♥ Read Genesis 22:16-18. What does God promise Abraham because of his obedience?

_____

_____

Abraham believes the Lord; the Lord declares him righteous because of his faith (Gen. 15:6). Abraham demonstrates his faith by his actions. He is willing to obey God even to the point of sacrificing his only son. You can read Genesis 22:1-16 to discover that God does this to test Abraham's faith and obedience. I cannot second-guess why God asks Abraham to sacrifice his son, but as we studied in previous lessons, testing usually is intended to build character or strengthen our commitment to our Heavenly Father. I also know that if we hold on to something too tightly, we may be asked to give it up, especially if it becomes more important to us than God.

♥ Read Romans 4:20-21. For what is Abraham noted?

_____

♥ For what do you want to be noted?

_____

Over and over again throughout the Scripture Abraham is remembered for his faith in God. He is convinced that God is able to do anything He promises; Abraham believes and trusts God. However, we also see that Abraham's life is an example of faith in action. Hebrews 11:8-10 reminds us that Abraham obeys when God tells him to leave his home and go to another land where God will give him an inheritance. He goes without knowing where he is going and lives as a foreigner in the Promised Land by faith because he believes that God will provide.

Someday you too may be asked to give up your secure surroundings to do the will of your Heavenly Father. If so, will you be willing to go? This happened to my husband and me. We believed that our Father told us to go to another country of which we had never heard and love a nation we did not know. In fact we even had to look it up on a map to see where the country was. In our wildest imagination we actually thought we were going to a desert, but things turned out quite differently. You see, it was actually an answer to prayer. My heart's desire was to someday live in the mountains of North Carolina when we retired, but our Father allowed our surroundings to change much sooner. So, we left for the other country. You can only imagine our surprise when we arrived and found ourselves in the middle of the tallest, most beautiful mountains I had ever seen with the deepest and steepest valleys I had ever looked down into. The mountainsides were perfectly terraced all the way down; the view was breathtaking. I cried with a heart full of emotion as I gazed from our home at the 360-degree view of those mountains. When we follow

His leadership as Abraham does in the Bible story, we have no regrets.

♥ **Read Galatians 3:6-9. Who do you believe are the real children of Abraham?**
_____

♥ **Read Galatians 3:24-29. How do you become a child of God?**
_____

According to Galatians the real children of Abraham are all those who put their faith in God. So does that mean as believers we are children of Abraham? Absolutely! We are children of God through faith in Jesus Christ. As true believers, we are one in Jesus, thus we are true children of Abraham. We are his heirs; now all the promises God gives to Abraham in the Scripture belong to us too. Wow!

Our Heavenly Father makes a promise to Abraham. In the Bible story He blesses Abraham by sending Jesus as one of his descendants. Our Heavenly Father never changes or breaks His promises. He assures us that He forgives us of our sins and saves us through faith in Jesus. We are His heirs in the promise of eternal life. Abraham's faith pleases God. Does yours? Abraham is justified by his works. Are you? Are you willing to obey and DO His will when He calls? God gives us a choice. Which one will you make? A *faith that works* desires to please God, to be justified by works, and to be willing to obey. Our Father's love is all encompassing; I owe Him my life. What about you?

--♥ ---
Work out what God works in.

Oswald Chambers

Your Thoughts

Questions

Comments

Prayer Requests

Prayer Answers

Week 3, Day 5

Rahab, a Woman of Action

Today's Focus: James 2:14, 17, 20, 25-26; Joshua 2:1-22; 6:22-25; Hebrews 11:31; Galatians 5:6; 6:4

Yesterday we looked at the life of Abraham and how his life is one of faith that is justified by his actions. Today we examine the life of Rahab, a known prostitute. My, what a contrast—the founder of the Jewish nation compared to a woman with a bad reputation! These two people are so very different, yet both become ancestors of the Lord Jesus. Both believe God and are justified by their actions that result from their faith. Rahab even is listed in the "Faith Hall of Fame" in Hebrews. Let's see what God's Word has to say about Rahab.

♥ **Read James 2:25-26. What actions do you think make Rahab right with God?**

_____

_____

♥ **Read Joshua 2:1-22. What risks do you believe Rahab takes when she hides the spies?**

_____

_____

James states that Rahab is made right with God by hiding the spies and sending them safely away by a different road. Rahab acknowledges that the . . . *Lord your God is the supreme God of the heavens above and the earth below* (Josh. 2:11). Evidently her faith is genuine as she is willing to risk her life to protect and help the spies. Joshua mentions that Rahab's house is built into the city wall and is used to provide lodging for travelers as well as providing "favors". Thus, her house is a natural place for hiding the spies; the location provides a way of escape over the wall.

♥ **Read Hebrews 11:31. Why do you think the lives of Rahab and her family are spared when Jericho is destroyed?**

_____

_____

Rahab has faith and trusts God to spare her and her family when Jericho is destroyed. She admits to having fear but does not allow her fear to affect her belief that God can save her. She does the right thing in protecting the spies. The fact that our Heavenly Father uses ordinary people regardless of our past or how others may see us is interesting to me. Just think about it: would you have chosen a prostitute to save the spies? I am so thankful that God sees our hearts and even our faith. The Scriptures paint Rahab as a very resourceful and courageous woman. Through her belief in God she rises above her profession. That tells me that we can do the same. No matter what our circumstances or fears are in life, with God's help we can rise above them through our trust in our Heavenly Father. Praise the Lord! How encouraging!

♥ **Read James 2:14, 17, and 20. What do you believe is the central theme of these three verses?**

_____

_____

_____

Three times James emphasizes that faith is essentially dead and useless if it doesn't show itself by good deeds or actions. James evidently believes with all of his heart that true faith changes our conduct and our thoughts. Perhaps as the half-brother of our Lord Jesus he sees that change in his own life. Perhaps he is speaking from experience as he stresses that deeds are not a replacement for our faith but a confirmation of our faith in Jesus. He cites Abraham and Rahab, two totally opposite individuals in every area, as examples of active obedience demonstrating that *true faith* is genuine. To James faith expresses itself in love (Gal. 5:6) and is a *faith that works* because it is confirmed by actions.

Are you willing to put on your action shoes? If so, make sure you do it for the right reasons. Be yourself and remember that the action must be in obedience to our Heavenly Father. Ask Him what He wants you to do! He will tell you. Each of us is different, as were Abraham and Rahab. Each of us must do what God calls us to do. Yet, we are alike in that we believe in the same Lord and that He wants us to be heirs to His kingdom. Therefore, for a *faith that works*, serve others, treat others fairly, and help others with good deeds. Are you ready? Let's go.

-- ♥ --

Thinking of others is the heart of Christ-likeness and the best evidence of spiritual growth . . . If I have no love for others, no desire to serve others, I should question whether Christ is really in my life.

Rick Warren

Be sure to do what you should, for then you will enjoy the personal satisfaction of having done your work well . . .

(Gal. 6:4).

Your Thoughts

Questions

Comments

Prayer Requests

Prayer Answers

Week 4
Characteristic 5:
Faith Controls the Tongue

Day 1
Talking Too Much

Day 2
Power of the Tongue

Day 3
An Evil Tongue

Day 4
Taming the Tongue

Day 5
Blessing and Cursing

Welcome to our fourth week of study. At the conclusion of this week we will have completed half of our study through the Book of James. I am so excited that you have committed to walk with me through these pages. As you notice, James seems to have a way of getting to the heart of the matter. From last week's study, we discovered several truths about putting actions to our faith. Those truths include:
- Faith is shown by expressing love to others through our actions.
- No good deed is ever useless.
- True believers are heirs to all God promises Abraham.
- Genuine faith results in a willingness to be obedient to our Heavenly Father.
- A *faith that works* is confirmed by actions.

This week we will focus on the *Fourth Characteristic of Faith: Faith Controls the Tongue*. We will explore ways of controlling and taming the tongue as well as what happens when a tongue is out of control. We will look at the differences in our speech as to who motivates it—Satan or our Heavenly Father. BIG DIFFERENCE!

Heart Truths
Day 1: James 3:2
Day 2: James 3:5
Day 3: James 3:6
Day 4: James 3:8
Day 5: James 3:10

Week 4, Day 1

Talking Too Much

Today's Focus: James 1:26; 3:1-2; Matthew 12:33-37; Acts 15:24; Proverbs 15:1-4; Romans 2:17-29.

In the first chapter of James we are cautioned to be quick to listen and slow to speak. In the second chapter of James we are told to put actions to what we hear God telling us to do. Now in this chapter James wants to show us how to be slow to speak and how to watch the doors of our mouths. Therefore, the next five days will focus on our tongues and our speech.

You have heard the expression, "Sticks and stones may break my bones, but words will never harm me." Well, that is a big FAT lie! I know this because some of the most painful experiences I have had were because of either my inconsiderate words or the words someone else spoke. Now this may be an assumption on my part, but I believe I am not the only one who has "opened mouth and inserted foot" or has had a painful experience because of someone else lashing out. So, today we will look at what happens when we talk too much and how we are judged for our speech. Let's see what James says.

♥ **Read James 3:1-2. Why do you think James admonishes the people about becoming teachers?**

_____

_____

In the Jewish culture teaching is an extremely valued and respected profession. It is considered the highest calling of a Jewish child. *Teacher* or *Rabbi* means power, privilege, and respect. Many desire to become teachers because this profession will raise them to a higher social status as well as make them appear more religious. However, James warns people not to become teachers, because doing so increases their responsibility and accountability to God; thus God will judge them more severely. James values teaching, but he knows that teachers' words and deeds influence the spiritual lives of others. What they say matters; what they don't say matters also. We do know that in New Testament times, many teachers weaken the truth about being saved by grace and do not live as they teach (Acts 15:24 and Rom. 2:17-29). Does that sound familiar today?

James also warns the people not to become teachers because they too easily can stumble. Now what does this mean? The word *stumble* means to trip on an obstacle or, in this case, to sin. We are all prone to mistakes, especially in our speech. Sometimes our mouths run faster than our minds do, then . . . *oops!* . . . out pop the words! None of us is perfect, but the ability to control the tongue is a true mark of Christian maturity.

♥ **Read Matthew 12:33-37. In these verses what do you think Jesus reminds you pertaining to your words?**

_____

_____

In these verses Jesus reminds us that whatever is in our hearts determines what we say. He says a good person produces good words from a good heart; an evil person produces evil words from an evil heart. Jesus also says that on judgment day we must give an account of every idle word we speak and that our words reflect our fate. Either we will be justified by our words or condemned by them. OUCH! Do you need to discover and inspect the kind of words that emerge from your mouth? What does this tell you? This tells me I need the help of the Holy Spirit to make my motives and attitudes right and good so that my speech will be clean and acceptable to my Heavenly Father. It also tells me that what is inside of me affects my speech; therefore, I had better be careful what I allow in! Let's look further.

♥ **Read James 1:26. What happens to you if you do not control your tongue?**

_____

_____

James says if we claim to be religious and do not control our tongues, we are only fooling ourselves and our religion is worthless. Does that mean we all are to control our speech more effectively? Of course it does. So how can we do that?

♥ **Read Proverbs 15:1-4. What are some ways that you can control your tongue?**

_____

_____

Proverbs tells us that harsh words stir up anger, but if we answer in a gentle, quiet way, we will diffuse anger. Proverbs also tells us that too many words become as foolishness, gentle words bring life and health, and a deceitful tongue will crush the spirit. So how can we control the tongue? We can speak softly and not yell or holler. We can use fewer words and not ramble on and on. We can think before we speak and not blurt out the first things that enter our minds. We can be gentle with our words and not harsh. We can speak the truth and not be deceitful or manipulative. Are you willing to do these things? I sure am, but I will need my Heavenly Father to help me!

♥ **Read Romans 2:21. What does this verse say you are to do?**

_____

_____

Paul says we are to teach ourselves if we teach others. What do you think he means by that? Simply stated, we are to practice what we preach. In New Testament times many teachers ignore what they taught. In other words, they are excusing their own actions while they criticize the actions of others. Does this sound familiar today? So, how do we recognize a true Christian teacher?

True Christian teachers model what they teach. They teach God's Truths, not just their own opinions or what they think people want to hear. True Christian teachers are people of integrity. Their lives and words match and are not in opposition. They do not say one thing and do another. True Christian teachers are not hypocritical in their actions or motives. If you desire to be a teacher or if you already are a teacher, then live your life without contradictions. Accept the responsibility to teach God's Truths. To be a true Christian teacher you have no choice. According to James teachers will be judged more severely. For a *faith that works*, control your tongue by not talking too much and by being careful about what you allow to enter your heart. Model what you teach! Are you willing?

Dearest Heavenly Father,
I pray that I would never be guilty of leading anyone astray. Please protect my mouth from speaking idle or foolish words. Control my words that they will be gentle and loving and kind in all situations. May I speak with Your words, hear with your ears, and see with your eyes. May the words of my mouth and the meditations of my heart be acceptable in your sight, for you, Oh, Lord, are my strength and my redeemer!
In Jesus name I pray, Amen

---♥--
The affairs of mankind are thrown into confusion
by the tongues of men.
Matthew Henry

Your Thoughts

Questions

Comments

Prayer Requests

Prayer Answers

Week 4, Day 2

Power of the Tongue

† **Heart Truths:**

So also the tongue is a small part of the body, and yet it boasts of great things. Behold, how great a forest is set aflame by such a small fire!
(Jas. 3:5 NAS).

Today's Focus: James 3:3-5; Psalms 32:9; 39:1; 141:3; Proverbs 16:28; 20:19; 25:23; 26:18-28; Colossians 3:5-11

In yesterday's study James lays the groundwork for our further discussion about the tongue. He stresses a stricter judgment for teachers, because "too much talk" leads to stumbling. Now don't think for one minute that this gets you off the hook if you are not a teacher, because it doesn't! James is saying that people who control their mouths will be able to control the rest of the body. So, my friend, this applies to ALL of us. We will be judged for all the words that proceed from our mouths. My, what a realization! Today James builds a case for the impending damage the tongue can do if it is not kept in check. The power of small things as they affect larger things is an incredible phenomenon. Let's see what James has to say.

♥ **Read James 3:3-5. What three analogies does James use to compare the power of the tongue?**

_____

_____

♥ **What do you think James is saying by using these analogies?**

_____

_____

James uses three analogies to make his point about the power of the tongue: (1) A large horse will go in any direction we want by means of a small bit in his mouth. (2) A tiny rudder will make a huge ship turn wherever the captain directs it to go. (3) A tiny spark can cause a great forest fire. I believe James is really trying to drive a point home, because he uses word pictures that will make an unforgettable impression on the persons to whom he writes. Think about it! A bit, a rudder, and a spark—all three are very small objects that control much larger objects. Thus, the same is true with the tongue. But what damage the tongue can do to us and to others if not controlled! People are said to open their mouths around 700 times a day to speak. Wow! That is a lot of potential times to stumble. Right?

♥ **Read Psalms 141:3. Why do you think David asks the Lord to keep his lips sealed?**

_____

_____

David, *a man after God's own heart*, cries out to the Lord to keep his lips sealed. Why do you believe he does that? Could he have had the same problem that possibly we all have about our tongues? David wants our Heavenly Father to guard what he says so that his words will bring honor and glory to Him. *Oh, Father, me too! Please, I need your control as much or more than did David.* What about you? Continue reading.

♥ **Read Psalms 32:9 and 39:1. What do these psalms tell you to do?**

_____

_____

That's right! Through David the psalms tell us to bridle our tongues to keep them under control. Funny how our Father describes some people as being like mules that need to be controlled by bits and bridles! However, this is not so funny when I look in the mirror and see that He could mean me. I think of times in which my stubbornness has gotten in the way and how my Father in heaven gently wooed me back. Even at times I had to have a bit in my mouth to listen to Him. Does He recognize our stubbornness and wants us to learn to be submissive and useful for Him?

♥ **Read Proverbs 26:18-28. Name some problem areas related to the tongue that these verses address.**

_____

_____

♥ **Read verse 20 again. What goes out from a lack of fuel?**

_____

_____

These verses address many of the sins of speech that an uncontrolled tongue produces. Some of these problem areas or sins mentioned are quarrels, gossip, rumors, burning words, and hatred. Other areas may include putting others down, bragging, manipulating, false teaching, exaggerating, complaining, and flattering. Do any of these ring a bell? You are not squirming, are you?

Proverbs has much to say about these areas. For example gossip separates the best of friends (Prov. 16:28), tells secrets (Prov. 20:19), and causes anger (Prov. 25:23). However, we are told that the fire goes out for lack of fuel and that quarrels disappear when gossip stops (Prov. 26:20). What do you think verse 20 means in relation to gossip or any other sin of speech for that matter? If you have ever played the "gossip" game, you know that everyone sits in a circle; one person whispers something in the ear of the next person. Then that "one something" is whispered around the circle until it returns to the person who first said it. The "one something" originally said is usually quite different than what is returned from those who passed it around in the circle. So I believe verse 20 is telling us not to pass that "one something" to anyone. If we refuse to discuss it, the fuel line will be cut off and the fire will die. Make sense? Sometimes a rumor or gossip has a life of its own and cannot be controlled. So be careful that what you speak is always the truth.

♥ Read Colossians 3:5-11. What does Paul tell you to put to death?

_____

_____

Words are damaging because they quickly spread destruction. Without controlling the tongue, destruction surely follows. Therefore, Paul tells us to get rid of and put to death the sins of speech—to strip off the old evil nature and put on the new clothes of the brand-new nature. As you learn more and more about Jesus, Who created this new nature within you, your new nature will be continually renewed. Sometimes we forget that Jesus, through the Holy Spirit, lives inside us as believers; that is what matters most. Let your conduct match your faith and control your tongue.

In a previous lesson I mentioned some tidbits about my dad. But I am again reminded that when he finally became a believer, a radical change occurred in him. Dad went from being a foul-mouthed sailor to a sweet-mouthed servant. Imagine that! Now don't think for one moment that his previous words did not hurt me, because I still have recurrent thoughts of all those trashy, foul-mouthed words. Especially when I get upset, those awful words flood back into my mind; I have to ask forgiveness immediately. I say this to remind you and me that what we say with our tongue has far-reaching effects and impacts those around us as well as those we may never even know. To have a _faith that works_, control your tongues. So always ask yourself, are your words necessary? Are they kind? Don't be afraid to put a bit in your mouth if you need to. _UGH!_ I know sometimes when I see that "mule" in the mirror, I have to put in a "bit." It really works, but it sure does make my mouth really sore!

---♥ --

Don't talk too much, for it fosters sins. Be sensible and turn off the flow
(Prov. 10:19).

What we say will not only affect others but will affect us!
Jill Briscoe

Your Thoughts

Questions

Comments

Prayer Requests

Prayer Answers

Week 4, Day 3

An Evil Tongue

Today's Focus: James 3:5-6; Matthew 15:11, 18-19; Psalms 73:8; 34:13; Proverbs 8:13; 16:18, 27

Yesterday we looked at the power of the tongue and how small things have an enormous influence on much larger things. Today we will continue that discussion as we observe James comparing the tongue to a raging fire and as we examine the damage the tongue is capable of doing. The tongue is one of Satan's most powerful weapons! He uses the tongue to divide us, to put us at odds with each other, to spread destruction, and to cause wounds so deep that without our Heavenly Father's help they would never heal. Just think about what your speech reflects if it is motivated by Satan.

♥ **Read Matthew 15:11, 18-19. When you read these verses, how did you respond to what Jesus says about your words and your heart?**

_____

_____

Jesus said we are not defiled by what goes into our mouths; instead, we are defiled by what we say and do. Jesus further says that evil thoughts produce evil words, murder, adultery, all sexual immorality, theft, lying, and slander. Everything starts in our minds and then emerges in our words! That is why Jesus warns us to have pure thoughts; we act out and say what we think about. Ouch! What we think and say is what makes us unclean. The old saying, "What comes in, goes out", is so true! Read further.

♥ **Read Psalms 73:8. What is the sin of which this verse speaks?**

_____

_____

That's right! When we witness people criticizing and speaking evil about others, this usually results from their pride. God's Word says, *Pride goes before destruction, and haughtiness before a fall* (Prov. 16:18). His Word also says, *All who fear the Lord will hate evil. That is why I hate pride, arrogance, corruption, and perverted speech* (Prov. 8:13). Many times we see people trying to make others look bad to make themselves look good. That doesn't work; that type of behavior will only backfire on the person doing it. However, we know that destructive words cause great harm because of the powerful force behind them. In fact James is right when he writes that words can be like a spark of fire: once they emerge, the damage cannot be controlled or reversed. Words have a "mind of their own" and can destroy.

♥ **Read Proverbs 16:27. What are your thoughts about who looks for scandal?**

_____

_____

Again we see that the Bible is very clear about the use of our words. Proverbs says scoundrels look for scandal; their words are a destructive blaze. But who is a *scoundrel*? A *scoundrel* is defined as a crook or a rascal — an offender. Have you ever offended anyone? I know I have, so does that make me a *scoundrel*? I may not have gone out hunting for a scandal or gossip, but how did I respond when it approached me? Did I, too, become guilty of being destructive? Let me share an experience with you even though it had nothing to do with a scandal.

Many years ago I had a dear friend; in fact, we were prayer partners together. She was so precious to me; I learned much from her about prayer. Through her example I learned how to really praise my Heavenly Father. Well, being the outspoken person that I am, one day I said something to her that must have hit her like a ton of bricks. In fact, during our conversation I actually could visualize her building a brick wall barrier between us. Even though the words I spoke were true, I do not believe she ever totally forgave me; consequently, our relationship was severed. I apologized, begged her forgiveness, and did everything I knew to do to restore it. But it was too late. The relationship that was so beautiful for many years was over. This hurt me deeply. Even now when I think about it, I get weepy, because, you see, I loved her like a sister and still do. So be careful what you speak. Sometimes, truth or not, a person may not be willing to accept your words. Satan knows just how to destroy a friendship. The tongue, that little old spark, in a moment has the ability to destroy all the good that has been built up over the years.

In God's Word we see that our speech is motivated by Satan when we have pride, selfish ambition, evil unspiritual thoughts, bitterness, envy, anger, and/or jealousy in our minds and hearts. That type of speech produces evil words, murder, adultery, all sexual immorality, theft, lying, and slander. For me to realize that a mean spirit or a critical word proceeding from my mouth can cause all of this damage is overwhelming. All I can plead is, "Father, forgive me!" Now that I feel like dirt itself, and maybe you do too, let's look at how we can overcome this sort of speech and put out that spark of fire.

♥ **Read Psalms 34:13. In this verse what do you think David advises you to do?**

_____

_____

David warns us to watch our tongues and to keep our lips from telling lies. Bottom line is that we are to obey our Heavenly Father in the way we use our tongues and in the words we speak. Please know we are never alone as we battle the evil of Satan. Remember, the battle is the Lord's, not ours, but we are expected to listen and obey His Holy Word. Our Heavenly Father does not overlook deception or any other sin of speech; however, He is present to go through it with us, to teach us, and to build our characters.

♥ **Read James 3:5-6. What do these verses mean to you when you think about what the tongue is capable of doing?**

_____

_____

James says the tongue can launch a blazing fire capable of destroying our lives as well as destroying the lives of those around us. He says the tongue is set on fire by hell itself—Satan. _Ugh!_ Quite naturally we react to the words of others. However, when some seek to destroy us, this hurts deeply, especially if it is from those who claim to know the same Lord as we do. It really is like walking through the fires of hell. One such example:

Several years ago, I was innocently accused of wrongdoing in the workplace. A friend warned me that a particular group was trying to trap me so that I would be discredited and dismissed. PTL, my Heavenly Father showed me how to deal with the matter. I was able to bring the entire situation to light with documented proof. However, that did not stop the accusers of their viciousness. The sad thing is that they believed they were doing this for the "right" reasons. Sometimes we can convince ourselves that our behavior is "godly" when actually Satan himself is using us. Always examine your motives; stay clean before the Lord. Our Heavenly Father will tell you if you are wrong, but first, be willing to listen to Him. Remember the words of James: words can ruin your life and the lives of those around you and can turn your life into a blazing fire. The problem with blazing fires is they destroy everything in their path.

In our lesson tomorrow we will delve into the subject of taming the tongue and what we can do to control our tongues. But for now pray, pray, pray, as the temptation to "wag" the tongue is so great! Our words can be like a deeply lodged bullet in the inner lobes of the brain; that bullet never can be removed. Even though the pain will lessen and even may go away, we have a constant awareness of its presence that will last forever. To have a *faith that works*, be willing to turn an evil tongue into a good tongue. As the Bible shows us, Jesus amazingly does not fight back. He only says, *"Father, Forgive them!"* What will you say?

---♥ ---

Your Thoughts

Questions

Comments

Prayer Requests

Prayer Answers

Week 4, Day 4

Taming the Tongue

Today's Focus: James 3:7-8; Genesis 1:28; Psalms 51:10; 140:3; Romans 3:13; 12:1-2; Proverbs 4:24; 10:19; 12:16, 25; 16:24; Proverbs 17:14; 25:15

As you have already studied during these past few days, the tongue is full of uncontrolled evil that must be harnessed. So what can we do about it? James says, *No one can tame the tongue.* If that is true, how do we deal with an uncontrolled tongue? Rather than getting all worked up about this, when I am in a dilemma or have questions such as this, I like to search God's Word for an answer. We already see the Bible has numerous passages on this very topic, so let's begin.

♥ **Read Genesis 1:28. As you study this passage, why do you think God gives man and woman "control" when He creates them in His own image?**

_____

_____

According to the creation account in Genesis, God gives man and woman control over the fish, the birds, and all the animals. To be in "control" of something is to have absolute authority over it. Our loving Heavenly Father "delegates" that authority to us. He not only expects us to have "control" over the fish, birds, and animals but also to take care of them. Now, I'm really interested in the fact that we can tame lions, tigers, and all kinds of animals and birds—even porpoises and whales—but when taming our own tongues are involved, we are helpless. Something is terribly wrong with this picture! Read on.

♥ **Read and compare Romans 3:13 with Psalms 140:3. Why do you think your tongue and speech are being compared to a snake and an open grave?**

_____

_____

In the psalms David asks God to protect him from those who would slander, because their tongues sting like a snake and poison drips from their lips. In Romans we hear Paul saying no one is good and that people's talk is foul like the stench from an open grave. Paul also says their speech is filled with lies and that the poison of a deadly snake drips from their lips. Oh, my, what word pictures!

Close your eyes and imagine with me a snake with fangs exposed and venom dripping ready to strike at you any moment. Now imagine the smell from an open grave. Not only are both pictures disgusting, they use our senses to signal danger to all who are in close proximity. Is that our tongues?

Wait a minute! Did I hear you correctly? Are you saying this does not apply to you? Surely you are not saying, "I am not so bad. In fact, I am a lot better than the person next door or at church." Let me ask you a few questions. Have you ever lied or hurt someone's feelings by your words or by the tone of your voice? Have you ever been bitter or revengeful towards anyone? Have you ever been angry with someone just because the person did not agree with you? Have you ever thought evil thoughts about someone? Well, if you—as I am—are guilty of any of the above, then you stand just as guilty as I do before a Holy God. Then if that is the case, you are a sinner just like I am and in need of a forgiving God. When we stand as guilty sinners before our loving Heavenly Father, remember: only through belief in Jesus can we be saved. We cannot do it on our own; we need help. The same is true with our tongue. We cannot control it on our own; we must have help from Jesus.

♥ **Read the following verses. Identify the advice these verses give about your speech.**

Proverbs 4:24

_____

Proverbs 10:19

_____

Proverbs 12:16

_____

Proverbs 12:25

_____

Proverbs 16:24

_____

Proverbs 17:14

_____

Proverbs 25:15

_____

The pages of Proverbs are full of excellent advice about our speech and controlling our tongues. Some of that advice includes: (1) We are to avoid all perverse talk and corrupt speech. (2) We are to listen more and talk less. (3) We are to remain calm when we are insulted. (4) We are to use kind and encouraging words to cheer up people. (5) We are to refrain from quarreling. (6) We are to use soft speech, because it crushes strong opposition. However, according to James, <u>we</u> as human beings cannot tame the tongue on our own; we need help. That help is from Jesus, our Lord, and His Holy Spirit. So how do we obtain His help?

♥ **Read Psalms 51:10. This verse speaks of asking God for a clean heart and a renewed right spirit. How does this relate to controlling your tongue?**

_____

_____

David asks God to create in him a clean heart and to renew a right spirit within him. We, too, should ask God to do the same for us. Our hearts and spirits being clean and right is important, because what proceeds from our hearts is spoken through our mouths. We also know that making ourselves happy rather than including our Heavenly Father is only natural. Now I didn't say doing this was easy, but I can say my heart and spirit frequently require a tuneup and even at times an overhaul! What about yours?

♥ **Read Romans 12:1-2. For what else are you to ask God?**

_____

_____

In Romans, Paul says to give your body to God and be a living and holy sacrifice. He warns us not to copy the behavior and customs of this world but instead to allow God to transform us into new people by changing how we think. Sometimes I think that I need more than an overhaul. Perhaps I need a whole new transmission when my mind is concerned. I know if I allow God to transform me and change the way I think, then I will know what God wants me to do and say. What about you? We both know that our Heavenly Father wants only what is best for us. He gave His Son, Jesus, for us. In return give your life back to Him. Then and only then can your tongue and speech be controlled.

Jesus is the one who can control and tame your tongue, but you can rely on the Holy Spirit to make it possible. The Holy Spirit conforms us, comforts us, and keeps us from lashing out at folks who hurt us. If we let Him, the Holy Spirit directs our thoughts and actions each day. The Holy Spirit gives you the peace that passes all understanding. But you have a part in all of this, too. Listen and obey. Read God's Word every single day, meditate on it, and memorize it. And last but not least, pray. Then you will be in submission to His authority, have a *faith that works*, and have a tongue that can be tamed. Look at Illustration 1, Who Is In Control?, from the Appendix, page 221. Decide who needs to be on your throne.

---♥ ---

No man can tame the tongue, but through the grace of God

Augustine

Your Thoughts

Questions

Comments

Prayer Requests

Prayer Answers

Week 4, Day 5

Blessing and Cursing

Today's Focus: James 3:9-12; Genesis 1:26-27; 12:3; Luke 6:43-45; Matthew 26:35, 69-75; Deuteronomy 11:26; 1 Corinthians 4:12; 10:31; Proverbs 10:20, 32; 12:18

Yesterday we studied about taming the tongue. We realized that as believers we have no power within ourselves to tame the tongue. Instead we are to submit to Jesus' control our tongues along with our speech. In other words we must have help to control our tongues. The choice to have that help is brought home vividly today as we reflect on the blessing and cursing that actually can proceed from our mouths. As believers we need constant discipline from our Heavenly Father to speak wisely. If you claim to be a Christian, control what you say, because it reflects on your Father and on your Lord and Savior, Jesus Christ. Let's see what James has to say.

♥ **Read James 3:9-12. To what conflict do you think James refers in these verses?**

_____

_____

_____

From this Bible story we learn that a big problem with contradictory speech must be occurring. We recognize that the same problem exists today. James says sometimes the tongue praises our Lord and Father; sometimes it breaks out into curses against those who have been made in the image of God. He refers to blessing and cursing that pour out of the same mouth. He plainly states that this is NOT right. So what is James really saying? Let's look at what these words mean.

According to the *Life Application Dictionary/Concordance, blessing* means to honor in worship and/or to offer approval or encouragement. *Cursing*, on the other hand, means to pronounce a sentence and/or condemnation or judgment on a person. Quite the opposite, wouldn't you say? Have you ever wondered why our speech seems so contradictory, especially when our words are encouraging in one sentence and often destructive in another?

♥ Read Genesis 12:3 and 1 Corinthians 4:12. How would you respond to what these verses are saying?

_____

_____

In Genesis the Lord tells Abraham that He will bless those who bless him and curse those who curse him. However, in Corinthians we are told to bless those who curse us. In Deuteronomy 11:26 God gives Israel the choice of a blessing or a curse. I'm amazed that the Israelites choose their own way and in so doing choose the curse. Such a brilliant people, but do you suppose they really didn't believe God would actually curse them if they were disobedient? Do you believe that these verses apply to us today? Of course they do. To choose God's way is to choose blessings; He will bless those who bless us. The same applies with our tongues; we can choose to bless or to curse. But therein lies the inconsistency . . . how can that be so? Let me ask you some questions:

Have you ever—
• been considerate to strangers but inconsiderate to your family?
• been cordial at work but verbally abusive to your spouse or children?
• looked spiritual on Sunday yet told suggestive stories the rest of the week?
• been helpful at Bible study but damaged someone's reputation with gossip?
• praised the Lord in one sentence and cursed someone in another sentence?
• gained from worship yet excused negative talk?
• accepted criticism but condemned someone else destructively?
• been an angel at church but a devil at home?

I believe that if I have been guilty of some of these things, perhaps you, too, have been squirming as I mentioned these questions, but we won't dwell there. Let's move on and see that even though these things are wrong, we may be in good company.

♥ Read Matthew 26:35, 69-75. In these verses what happens to Peter?

_____

_____

Poor Peter. Can you relate? I surely can. In these verses we see Peter claiming that he never will deny Jesus; then only a few verses later Peter denies Jesus three times. This is just one example of the inconsistency and contradictory nature of our speech. Please realize I am not trying to excuse our behaviors or our speech; however, realize that inconsistent and contradictory speech happens to all of us. If that is true, then how do we deal with this behavior about the tongue and speech? Let's look further.

♥ Read Luke 6:43-45. When you read this example of the fig tree, how do you think you can apply it to your life?

_____

_____

Just as a tree is recognized by the fruit it produces, so believers are recognized by the fruit we produce. A good person produces good fruit from a good heart; an evil person produces evil fruit from an evil heart. Scripture says that whatever is in our hearts determines what we say with our tongues. Just as a tree does not produce both good and bad fruit nor does a spring of water produce both fresh and salty water, we are to avoid producing blessing and cursing from the same mouth. So why do we have such a struggle with our speech when we try so diligently? Is this because we have not asked Jesus to help us?

♥ Read Proverbs 10:20 and 10:32. If your words are to be like sterling silver, then what has to take place in your life for that to happen?

_____

_____

According to Proverbs the words of the godly (that's you and me if we are true believers) are like sterling silver and are helpful. First Corinthians 10:31 says, _Whatever you eat or drink or . . . do, you must do all for the glory of God._ Could we paraphrase that verse to read, _Whatever we say or do, we must say or do for the glory of God_? All this is about bringing glory to our Heavenly Father. No matter what we say or do, we can ask ourselves, "Father, will this glorify You?" If not, don't say it or do it! Then and only then will our words be helpful and become like sterling silver. I challenge you, as well as myself, to be consistent and congruent with your tongue and speech and not have both blessing and cursing spewing from your mouth.

Since we are made in the image of God (Gen. 1:26-27) and we are to reflect God's glory, let us fill our hearts with those things that are pure and lovely in His sight. Let us choose our words carefully and be quick to listen and slow to speak (Jas. 1:19). Let us ask ourselves if our words are necessary and kind. Let us remember that words can become a blazing fire, so we must be careful with sparks. Let us be in submission to Jesus' authority so our tongues can be tamed. And finally let us choose only blessing and never cursing. Folks, a _faith that works_ must bless and never curse.

-- ♥ ---

. . . Words of the wise bring healing

(Prov. 12:18).

Depending on Divine grace, let us take heed to bless and curse not,
and let us aim to be consistent in our words and actions

Matthew Henry

Your Thoughts

Questions

Comments

Prayer Requests

Prayer Answers

Week 5
Characteristic 5:
Faith Produces Wisdom

Day 1
Understanding God's Ways

Day 2
Bitter Jealousy and Selfish Ambition

Day 3
Earthly Wisdom

Day 4
Heavenly Wisdom

Day 5
Peacemakers

The study this week is so exciting for me. It is about WISDOM—a quality for which I have prayed almost every day of my life. I also have prayed that each of my children as well as my husband be granted wisdom—not earthly wisdom but the divine wisdom that originates with our Holy God. As I have prayed for wisdom, our Heavenly Father has revealed much of Himself to me, because my actual prayer is to see as He sees, to hear as He hears, and to speak as He speaks. My greatest desire in this life is to do the will of my Father in Heaven. However, to be able to do His will, understanding about Him and His ways is important. Therefore, this week's adventure of *Characteristic Five: Faith Produces Wisdom* will take us on a journey of understanding God's ways as we contrast earthly wisdom with divine wisdom and conclude with the blessings of being a peacemaker. So, get comfortable, pull up your chair, and let's begin. By the way, thank you for joining me through this adventure. I really do appreciate your presence.

Heart Truths
Day 1: James 3:13
Day 2: James 3:14
Day 3: James 3:15
Day 4: James 3:17
Day 5: James 3:18

Week 5, Day 1

Understanding God's Ways

Today's Focus: James 3:13; Isaiah 40:12-31; 55:8-9; Habakkuk 3:6; Psalms 18:30; 31:19; 86:11; 103:7; 145:17; Romans 5:8; 11:33; 12:3; Revelation 15:3; 2 Chronicles 1:1-12; 9:22-24; Matthew 6:22; Genesis 39-41; Jeremiah 31:3; Ephesians 2:4; Exodus 34:6

In our study last week we discovered that a *faith that works* is a faith in which the tongue is controlled at all times. We recognized that help from Jesus is necessary for us to have control over our tongues. We realized our need for His divine help, since from a human standpoint, this task is impossible to perform. I'm interested in the fact that immediately after he focuses on the importance of controlling the tongue, James emphasizes the need for a faith that produces wisdom. Could a relationship exist between wisdom and controlling the tongue? We will find out as we compare earthly wisdom with divine wisdom and discuss topics such as bragging, bitter jealousy, and selfish ambition. However, to understand true wisdom, understanding God's ways is important. And to understand God's ways, understanding Who God really is also is important. So, with that in mind, let's begin our study.

♥ **Read James 3:13. After you read this verse about what happens if you are wise and understand God's ways, write down the ways this verse can apply to your own life.**

_____

_____

James begins this section of his book by saying that if we are wise and understand God's ways, we will live lives of steady goodness so that only our good deeds will pour forth. He also emphasizes that if we do not brag about the good we do, we then will be truly wise! What does James mean? What is wisdom? What are God's ways? How do God's ways apply to our lives? Dig a little deeper with me.

The Greek word for <u>wisdom</u> is *sophia*, pronounced *sof-ee-ah*. It means that a person who is wise has the ability to discern right from wrong. A wise person is said to have moral sense, discretion, and sound judgment. Therefore, true wisdom is measured by a person's character and is exemplified by love, order, goodness, and peace. James says if we are wise, we will understand God's ways. So how do we gain the wisdom to understand God's ways? Let's look at who God is.

♥ Read the following verses. As He is being described, identify Who God is to you.

Ephesians 2:4

_____

Jeremiah 31:3

_____

Romans 5:8

_____

Exodus 34:6

_____

Psalms 31:19

_____

Isaiah 40:12-31

_____

To understand who God really is, read His Holy Word. From Ephesians, Jeremiah, and Romans, we discover that God loves and that His love is great, everlasting, and sacrificial. From Exodus and Psalms we identify God's glory, which is abundantly revealed in His infinite mercy, grace, and goodness. From Isaiah we recognize that God is all-powerful and that His power is manifested in creation, miracles, and the resurrection. Yet the all-powerful, almighty God cares for each of us personally.

Sometimes words are lacking to give our Heavenly Father the honor and glory He so rightly deserves. We also ascertain that our Holy God is all-knowing (1 John 3:20) as well as everpresent (Ps. 139:7-12). No one will ever compare to our Holy, infinite, sovereign God, Who chose to reveal Himself in His Son, Jesus Christ. He is Creator and Sustainer, the Alpha and the Omega. He is unchangeable, unequaled, incomparable, and the wisest of all. He is goodness, love, mercy, truth, and justice all combined into one. In Him we exist and have our being. To me God is my Heavenly Father. This is only a small glimpse of who our God really is, but let's look further and try to understand His ways.

Again we have to go to the Holy Scripture to understand what God's ways are. Let's look at the following verses.

♥ **Read the following verses and identify how God's ways are being described to you:**

Psalms 18:30

_____

Psalms 86:11

_____

Psalms 103:7

_____

Psalms 145:17

_____

Isaiah 55:8-9

_____

Habakkuk 3:6

_____

Romans 11:33

_____

Revelation 15:3

_____

In getting a glimpse of Who our God really is, we will try and understand that His ways are perfect, knowledgeable, righteous, everlasting, inscrutable, and true. We learn from the psalms that our Heavenly Father provides a protective shield for us, demonstrates kindness and mercy toward us, and teaches us His ways to give us a pure heart. We realize we can believe His promises because they are true. God wants us to ask Him to reveal Himself to us as He did to Moses. From Isaiah we understand that His ways and thoughts are not like our ways and thoughts because they are far greater and higher than ours. Hallelujah! From Habakkuk we identify God's everlasting power. From Romans we determine His ways to be wise and filled with ultimate knowledge and understanding. Even Revelation points out that His ways are just and true. Wow! How awesome are the ways of our Heavenly Father! I just wonder if we can possibly have only a small portion of the wisdom and ways of God. What do you think? Let's examine the lives of a couple of folks and see.

♥ **Read Genesis 39, 40, and 41. What happens in Joseph's life that demonstrates the ways of God?**

_____

_____

♥ **What has happened in your life that demonstrates the ways of God?**

_____

_____

♥ **Do you relate to Joseph? If so, in what way?**

_____

Most of us are familiar with the life of Joseph and his experience of being sold into slavery by his brothers when he is 17. However, we know that by age 30 Joseph is exalted over Egypt. So what happens during those 13 years between being sold and being exalted? In Genesis we find that Joseph experiences many trials and testing. He is tempted by a married Egyptian woman, unjustly thrown into prison, and ignored after interpreting the dreams of the chief cupbearer and chief baker. After several years of what must have been quite a "character-building" time, Joseph is called to interpret Pharaoh's dream and becomes exalted. Through his experiences of trials and testing God reveals His ways to Joseph and gives him the wisdom he needs to be a great leader. All of this happens because Joseph continues to trust in God. Does that mean when we undergo trials and testing yet continue to trust God, He will show us His ways and give us wisdom too? Yes, it means just that! Now let's take a look at the life of Solomon.

♥ **Read 2 Chronicles 1:1-12 and 9:22-24. What is Solomon's greatest desire?**

_____

_____

♥ **What is God's response to Solomon's desire?**

_____

_____

♥ **What is your greatest desire?**

_____

♥ **Have you asked God for it? Why or why not?**

_____

Solomon seeks the Lord; God appears to Solomon in a dream to ask him what he wants. Solomon asks God to give him wisdom and knowledge to rule the people properly. This request pleases God very much because as king, Solomon is concerned for the needs of his people rather than riches for himself. Therefore, not only does God grant the request, but He also adds riches, wealth, and honor. So what do we learn from this story? Could that same wisdom be available for us today? Of course it is, but first we must ask. Then we must dedicate ourselves to studying and applying God's Word. His Word, along with our prayers, is the source of divine wisdom. In Scripture we are told to "*seek first His kingdom and His righteousness; and all these things shall be added to you*" (Mt. 6:33, NAS). Folks, it all goes back to what our priorities are. Just like Solomon and Joseph, if we put our Heavenly Father first, others second, and ourselves last, He will grant us wisdom and show us His ways. But He expects us to ask.

The second part of James 3:13 stresses that to be truly wise, we are not to brag about the good we do. So what does *brag* mean? According to the *Life Application Dictionary, brag* means to boast or be prideful. I do not believe James is talking about a healthy self-esteem, because we are told in God's Word that we are to love others as ourselves; however, if we overestimate ourselves, then that becomes a problem and is considered to be prideful. Let's look at the following verse.

♥ **Read Romans 12:3. Look at what Paul is telling you in this verse. Decide how you can apply it to your life.**

_____

_____

Paul warns us to be honest in our estimations of ourselves and to measure our value by how much faith God has given us. What does that tell you? It tells me my example and identity are to be in Jesus. That means we are not to be evaluating ourselves according to earthly standards but only by eternal standards. Then and only then will we be truly wise. Let's look at one more verse.

♥ **Read Matthew 6:22. What kind of vision do you need?**

_____

_____

According to Jesus our eyes are the windows to our souls; therefore, we need pure eyes to let the sunshine into our souls. The only way we can see clearly is to have God's spiritual eyes. This means we cannot be self-serving or boastful, because that will only cloud our vision like a cataract does. For clear eyes we must keep our focus fixed on Jesus and our Heavenly Father. I believe it goes back to the reflection we see in the mirror. We must be honest with ourselves. When our

Heavenly Father says to fix something in our lives, we must be obedient and do it. However, if we become defensive, then perhaps we have a pride issue we need to deal with. To shield against being prideful of your talents or the abilities God has given you, be willing to use them in a humble way without bragging. So wisdom involves both our actions and our attitudes. What is that mirror telling you? To have a *faith that works*, we would be wise to know who God is and to understand His ways. But to be truly wise, be careful not to brag about the good you do.

--♥--

If any of you lacks wisdom, let him ask of God, who gives to all men (and women) generously and without reproach, and it will be given to him (and her)

(Jas. 1:5 NAS).

Your Thoughts

Questions

Comments

Prayer Requests

Prayer Answers

Week 5, Day 2

Bitter Jealousy and Selfish Ambition

Today's Focus: James 3:14-15; Genesis 3:1-6; 13:7-8; 1 Samuel 18:8; 2 Samuel 5:12; Philippians 2:3; Romans 13:13-14; Ephesians 4:31-32

As I examined bitter jealousy and selfish ambition, I became very uncomfortable. In fact when I researched the Scriptures, I somehow felt as though I was trying to make a case that did not exist. So I prayed. Wow! What a difference! My Heavenly Father immediately opened my eyes and showed me Scripture after Scripture about these two sinful problems that I am convinced, more than ever, are inspired by Satan. Now what do you think made the difference? Do you think that perhaps Satan did not want me to delve into his territory? Or was it because I was trying to do this particular lesson on my own rather than with my Father's inspiration? Actually, I think both things happened. I believe as we progress through the lesson today you will understand what I mean. In our focal verses, James is quick to warn us not to have bitter jealousy and selfish ambition in our hearts (Jas. 3:14-15). So, let's examine these two problems.

♥ **In your own words, what do you believe about the meaning of the following phrases:**

bitter jealousy

_____

_____

selfish ambition

_____

_____

The Greek word for *bitter* is *pikros*, pronounced *pik-ros*. It means sharp or pungent. *Easton's Bible Dictionary* says that *bitterness* is symbolic of affliction, misery, and servitude. We are warned that a *root of bitterness* becomes a dangerous sin (Heb. 12:15). From life experiences we know that *bitterness* causes resentment, anger, and hostility which eventually will destroy us. But what happens when the word *bitter* is used along with *jealousy*? The Greek word for *jealousy* is *zelos*, pronounced *dzay'-los*, and means zeal. We recognize a definite contrast with the word

104

jealousy when it is used favorably to mean the "indignant jealousy of God" as contrasted to the unfavorable use to mean envy. Perhaps the meaning is even stronger when *bitter* is used together with *jealousy*. Easton calls *jealousy* an intense interest or desire for another's honor or prosperity. When the words are put together, *bitter jealousy* becomes misguided zeal that results in anger at the accomplishments of other people.

♥ **Read Genesis 13:7-8. If you had a similar problem, what do you think bitter jealousy would do to you?**

_____

_____

In the scenario between the herdsmen of Abram and Lot we observe jealousy tearing them apart when instead they would have been better off pulling together against their hostile neighbors. As you know, this happens to believers today. Instead of unity we see believers bickering and being pulled apart as Satan works all around them. Jealousy is a driving force that is strong enough to tear apart the closest of friends. Bitter jealousy damages trust and peace, causes anger and bad tempers, prevents progress toward goals, and makes us self-centered and self-seeking rather than God-centered and God-loving. Let's look at the following:

♥ **Read 1 Samuel 18:8. What happens to Saul's attitude about David?**

_____

_____

♥ **Have you ever had a problem with bitter jealousy either toward another person or another person toward you? If so, what did you do about it?**

_____

_____

In 1 Samuel we observe Saul's appreciation for David turn to raging jealousy as the people sing about and celebrate David's accomplishments. Saul becomes obsessed with trying to have David murdered. His bitter jealousy becomes a cancer that controls Saul's life and produces sin. Satan uses jealousy to produce resentment; this manifests itself in seeking to harm or destroy another person. Beware, my friend! Don't allow jealousy to get a foothold in your life! So how do we prevent it?

♥ **Read Romans 13:13-14. What are you to do to prevent jealousy or other evils from controlling you?**

_____

_____

Paul warns us not to think of ways to indulge our evil desires. Instead we are to be decent and true in all we do and let the Lord Jesus take control of our lives. Paul knows that attitude is as important as actions are, thus he lists jealousy right along with drunkenness and immorality. Evidently he realizes that jealousy leads to fighting just as lust leads to adultery. But how do we allow Jesus to take control of our lives?

♥ **Read Ephesians 4:31-32. What do these verses tell you to do?**

_____

_____

♥ **How did you respond to these verses?**

_____

_____

Once again Paul warns us to get rid of all bitterness, rage, anger, harsh words, slander, and all types of malicious behavior. Instead we are to be kind to each other, tenderhearted, and forgiving of one another, just as God through Jesus forgives us. We allow Jesus to take control of our lives when we exemplify His love, humility, truth, and service. In other words in any given situation perhaps we should ask ourselves, "What would Jesus do?" Actually that is a pretty sound biblical truth and the best way I know of preventing bitter jealousy. Now let's take a look at the second problem that James warns us about—selfish ambition.

According to Torrey's _New Topical Textbook_, _selfishness_ is contrary to God's law and is condemned by Jesus. The actual word _selfish_ means self-centered, self-seeking, and self-interested. Torrey emphasizes that God and Jesus condemn ambition, especially if it is motivated by selfishness. The word _ambition_ can have both positive and negative meanings: positive, if one works toward a goal or dream and aspires to accomplish an objective with the right heart attitude; negative, if used together with _selfish_ producing the problem of selfish ambition, which is the desire to live only for one's self. "Selfish ambition" often manifests itself in manipulating things or people. Let's look at what "selfish ambition" can cause.

♥ **Read Genesis 3:1-6. From these verses we see that Satan is the one who inspires selfish ambition. How do you respond to that?**

_____

♥ **Please share a personal experience about the selfish ambition of someone you know.**

_____

_____

♥ What did you learn from this experience?

_____

_____

You are all familiar with the Genesis story of Adam and Eve's sin, but let's look for a minute to who inspires the sin and how he manages to do it. We notice Satan encouraging Eve to disobey God and to eat the fruit. He does so by making her think what she is doing is good and not evil. Satan tells her that if she eats the fruit, she will become just like God; this produces a selfish desire within her. In other words Satan manipulates Eve's desires for his purposes. Therefore, we recognize that selfish ambition produces sin (Acts 8:18-24), causes quarrels (Jas. 4:1-2), and becomes a pride issue (Isa. 14:12-15). Isn't that what happens to us today when we fall into the "me" pattern instead of looking to our Lord and Savior, Jesus? Read further.

♥ Read Judges 9:1-6. How did you react to what Abimelech does to get his own way?

_____

_____

In the passage Abimelech desires more than anything to be king of Israel and is evidently willing to do anything to make it happen. He is power-hungry, ruthless, and even has approximately 70 of his half-brothers killed to accomplish his purpose. Because of his selfish ambition he manipulates his relatives and takes advantage of his father's position to get his own way. People with selfish ambition often seek to fulfill their desires in ruthless ways. Isn't this what happens today? We can examine our ambitions to see if they are God-centered or self-centered. So how is ambition kept under control?

♥ Read 2 Samuel 5:12. When you read that the Lord makes David king for the sake of the people, how did you respond?

_____

David realizes that the Lord is the One Who makes him king over Israel and that he is king for the sake of the people and not for himself. David seeks God to help him keep his ambition under control. He acknowledges God and gives God first place in his life. He is willing to serve the people according to God's purposes and not his own. What is your true ambition? What is your attitude about ambition? Is it to seek greatness from God or from people? What or who is the driving force in your own life?

♥ Read Philippians 2:3. What are you to do to avoid selfish ambition?

_____

_____

According to Philippians we are not to be selfish nor try to make a good impression on others. Instead we are to be humble and to think of others as better than ourselves. Selfishness not only can ruin our own lives but can ruin the lives of others. We must lay aside selfishness and treat others with respect and love. Looking to Jesus, He is our best example of humility and selflessness. To me that says it all and is the best antidote I know for selfish ambition.

From our study today we realize that bitter jealousy and selfish ambition are inspired by Satan and must not get a foothold in our lives. Sometimes we can be drawn into these evil desires by well-meaning Christians who unknowingly allow Satan to use them. Therefore, do not deny the truth and be very aware that the deceiver, the "father of lies", can manipulate us into thinking wrong thoughts and then acting on them. Consequently, to have a _faith that works_, be careful not to harbor any bitter jealousy or selfish ambition in your heart; look to your Heavenly Father to help you have pure thoughts and motives.

---♥ --

Beware of any belief that makes you self-indulgent; it came from the pit, no matter how beautiful it sounds.

Oswald Chambers

Your Thoughts

Questions

Comments

Prayer Requests

Prayer Answers

Week 5, Day 3

Earthly Wisdom

Today's Focus: James 3:15-16; Galatians 5:19-21; Romans 2:8; 1 Corinthians 2:14; 3:3; 3:19; Matthew 4:1-11

Yesterday we spent our time discussing bitter jealousy and selfish ambition. Today and tomorrow we will continue that discussion as we compare the differences between earthly wisdom and heavenly wisdom. The Book of James is very emphatic about the problems jealousy and selfish ambition cause. James warns us we will find disorder and every kind of evil when these two sinful problems exist, because they are motivated by Satan (Jas. 3:15-16). Without further comment let's examine what God's Word has to say on the subject of earthly wisdom.

♥ **Read Galatians 5:19-21. What will be produced if you follow the desires of your sinful nature?**

_____

_____

♥ **Examine your own life. Have you had to deal with any evil desires? If so, were you able to overcome and learn from the experience?**

_____

_____

♥ **What do you believe are the consequences for those who follow the desires of their sinful natures?**

_____

_____

In these verses and following Paul contrasts the desires of our sinful natures with the *fruit of the spirit* that begin to develop in us when we become followers of Jesus. On Day Four we will discuss these heavenly qualities, but for now let's identify what is produced in us if we follow the desires of our sinful natures. According to God's Word the sinful nature produces evil results such as sexual immorality, impure thoughts, eagerness for lustful pleasure, idolatry, demonic activities, hostility, quarreling, jealousy, outbursts of anger, selfish ambition, divisions, arrogance, pride, envy, drunkenness, wild parties, and other kinds of sin.

Notice that Paul calls all of these desires *SIN*. The consequences of these sins are that we will not inherit the Kingdom of God. OUCH! This is serious, dear friends. All of us have evil desires. Ignoring them is very difficult at times. However, for you to win the battle over these desires, crucify them and give them to Jesus as well as ask the Holy Spirit for His guidance. Once again we have a choice and a decision to make. Either we deal with these desires and inherit the Kingdom of God, or we ignore them, or even worse, refuse to deal with them and NOT inherit the Kingdom of God. What is your choice? I know what mine is. Read further.

♥ **Read 1 Corinthians 3:3. How do you act if you are controlled by your sinful desires?**

_____

_____

Paul calls us *immature believers* if we are still controlled by our own sinful desires. He further states if we are jealous of each other and quarrel with each other, we are acting like people who are not believers and do not belong to the Lord. The evidence of immaturity is that the people are quarreling like children and allowing their jealousy to separate them. Immature believers are controlled by their own desires, whereas mature believers have the desires of our Heavenly Father. Have you ever asked yourself, *Who controls my desires?* If your answer is *me*, then be careful, because your growth as a believer will be repressed!

♥ **Read 1 Corinthians 2:14. From this verse what truth do you identify?**

_____

_____

According to these verses people who are not Christians cannot understand the truths from God's Spirit because they sound like foolishness to them. Only those of us who have the Spirit can understand what the Spirit is saying and means. This is an important truth to know, because you cannot expect most people to understand your decision to follow Jesus. It seems silly to them. If people reject Jesus, they simply will not understand. They cannot hear what our Heavenly Father is saying when the lines of communication are broken.

♥ **Read Romans 2:8. Our Heavenly Father says He will pour out his anger on those who live for their own sinful desires. Do you know someone who you believe has experienced God's anger and wrath as a result of sinful desires? If so, what happened?**

_____

_____

_____

Our Heavenly Father will pour out His anger and wrath on those who live for themselves, who refuse to obey the truth, and who practice evil deeds. This verse reminds me of a young man I knew many years ago. He was a sweet, handsome young man, but he constantly was getting into trouble. He was into all sorts of evil stuff—from drugs to sex. He would not listen to anyone, especially his parents, who seemed to have no control over him. One unfortunate day when he was an older teen-ager, he dived into a river from a bridge and became paralyzed from his neck down. Was this God's anger and wrath on this young man? Was this to teach him a lesson? I cannot second-guess my Heavenly Father, but I can observe what He did allow to happen.

♥ Read Matthew 4:1-11. In the passage how does Jesus overcome Satan's temptations?

_____

_____

Many of you are familiar with the temptations of Jesus and how Jesus wisely combats Satan with Scripture verses. Not only does Satan tempt Jesus, he constantly fights against those of us who follow and obey Jesus. Satan wants to block God's purpose for our lives; he will use any means that he can. He uses temptations that are combined with real needs and possibly doubts to create inappropriate or evil desires. Satan also tempts us by using our strengths to make us become prideful or self-righteous. Always be alert and aware of your weaknesses as well as your strengths to combat all evil desires. When you are tempted, turn to Jesus and God's Word for strength to overcome.

♥ From your own experiences how has Satan tempted you through your strengths?

_____

_____

♥ Read 1 Corinthians 3:19. How do you think God views earthly wisdom?

_____

_____

♥ How are you to view earthly wisdom?

_____

Paul warns the Corinthians not to glory in earthly wisdom, because God's ways and thoughts are far above ours. Evidently the Corinthian believers are bragging about the wisdom of their leaders and teachers. They appear to be valuing the person rather than the message. Consequently we see that God views the wisdom of this world as foolishness. We also observe our Heavenly Father entrapping those who think they are wise in their own cleverness.

From today's study we understand Satan's deception and how he tries to manipulate us into sinful evil desires disguised as earthly wisdom. However, I also want you to understand that sometimes we are ineffective in our lives because we are confused about what our Heavenly Father wants for us. Confusion originates from Satan. So to avoid Satan's confusion, study God's Word carefully and listen to what our Heavenly Father says through His Word, through prayer, through other believers, and through circumstances. Once again, to have a *faith that works*, be careful to watch out for your vulnerabilities and to avoid earthly wisdom.

What a heavy lesson! Thanks for hanging in there with me. Cheer up! The other half of the contrast between earthly and heavenly wisdom brings joy. Tomorrow we will discover how to further cope with keeping evil desires at bay.

--♥ --

To be as immovable as a pillar in the house of our God, is an end for which one would gladly endure all the shakings that may be necessary to bring us there!

Hannah Whitall Smith

Your Thoughts

Questions

Comments

Prayer Requests

Prayer Answers

Week 5, Day 4

Heavenly Wisdom

Today's Focus: James 3:17; 1:5; Proverbs 2:1-6; 2:9-10,12; 3:13-18; Proverbs 4:7; 8:12; 9:1,10,11; Galatians 5:22-23

During the past two days we have spent time studying about the earthly wisdom Satan produces. Today will be a total contrast as we focus on the godly wisdom from our Heavenly Father. That wisdom is available to all believers as a gift if we will ask Him for it. By seeking heavenly wisdom we will discover that it will deliver us from selfish ambition, bitter jealousy, and other satanic sins. Let's begin our study by understanding exactly what heavenly wisdom really is.

♥ **In your own words how would you define and describe *heavenly wisdom*?**

_____

_____

Heavenly wisdom means practical discernment or applied truth from God. According to the *Life Application Dictionary/Concordance*, it is the ability to discern right from wrong and is based on God's Truth. That means true wisdom originates from God and begins with honor and respect for our Heavenly Father. So how do we get it?

♥ **Read James 1:5. What does James say you are to do if you want wisdom?**

_____

_____

According to James if we need wisdom and want to know what God wants us to do, then ask Him. He will gladly tell us and will not resent our asking. As believers we can pray to our Heavenly Father. We can have the assurance He will generously give us wisdom to guide our choices, our decisions, and our needs. We do not have to fumble around in the dark. Our Father is there for us, but we must ask to receive.

♥ **Read Proverbs 2:9-10. What will you understand when you receive wisdom?**

_____

_____

Wisdom is a lifelong process that is acquired only through reverence for and fear of God. Wisdom begins with trusting, respecting, and honoring our Heavenly Father (Prov. 9:10). Then we realize we have to first ask Him for wisdom with the understanding that the Holy Scriptures also reveal God's wisdom to us if we will read them (Prov. 8:12). As we heed and listen to our Heavenly Father through prayer and through the Scriptures, we learn the difference between right and wrong, because we know He will show us the right course of action every time. Lastly, we avoid moral pitfalls and sinful blunders because hopefully we have learned from our mistakes. My grandfather, Ben, used to say, "Learn from the mistakes of others, because you will not live long enough to make them all yourself." This is very wise yet practical advice for all of us to heed.

♥ **Read Proverbs 2:3-6. As you read these verses, what are some ways you can find wisdom?**

_____

_____

To find wisdom listen to what your Heavenly Father is saying through His Word. Cry out and intensely search for insight and understanding. Then you will understand what fearing the Lord and gaining His wisdom and knowledge means. In other words realize wisdom is a gift from God; however, you have to search for it to find it. That takes persistence, but the rewards and benefits are worth the effort.

♥ **Read Proverbs 3:13-18. Receiving heavenly wisdom has several benefits. What are some of the benefits that you want to apply to you?**

_____

_____

According to Proverbs the person who finds heavenly wisdom gains understanding and is happy. Wisdom is better than silver or gold and more precious than rubies. It will guide us down delightful paths and give us a long, prosperous life (Prov. 9:11). Wisdom will grant us favor with God and people and will give us a reputation for good judgment (Prov. 8:12), help us succeed and lack nothing (Prov. 9:1), and protect us from evil individuals (Prov. 2:12). We can be confident that wisdom ultimately will lead to blessings from our Heavenly Father. PTL!

♥ **Read James 3:17. What qualities do you think will be yours if your wisdom originates from heaven?**

_____

_____

James says that godly wisdom is pure, peace-loving, gentle, considerate of others, submissive, merciful, produces good deeds, impartial, and always sincere. Along with the benefits Proverbs mentions, why would anyone want earthly wisdom over heavenly wisdom?

♥ **Read Proverbs 4:7. According to this verse what is the most important thing you can do?**

_____

♥ **How did you respond to this verse?**

_____
_____

According to the Bible, David teaches Solomon from his childhood that seeking God's wisdom is the most important thing his son can do. Thus, the first thing Solomon does when he becomes king is to seek wisdom from God. Solomon is known as the wisest man who ever lived. His father, David, is also wise enough to never allow his failures to keep him from the worship of God, Who is the source of wisdom. Even Abigail, who eventually becomes David's wife, is wise in managing her household in spite of a very mean-spirited husband. We, too, can make God's wisdom the most important thing we can ask for through prayer . . . because we know our loving Heavenly Father will grant our request if we ask!

What is your choice? Do you put on your sinful nature which results in disorder and the evil actions of earthly wisdom inspired by Satan? Or, do you put on heavenly wisdom which results in the good fruit of righteous actions? We know that through the abiding presence of the Holy Spirit we will produce the very character traits that our Lord Jesus manifests in _love, joy, peace, patience, kindness, goodness, faithfulness, gentleness, and self-control_ (Gal. 5:22-23). However, we all have a choice! What is yours?

Have you prayed for God to exemplify heavenly wisdom in your life? If not, why not? It is yours for the asking. Almost every day of my life I have prayed for godly wisdom, because if I am on my own, I really know how to make a BIG mess of things! To have a _faith that works_ ask for and put on heavenly wisdom. After you have had time to peruse Chart 3, "Earthly Wisdom versus Heavenly Wisdom" on page 220 of the Appendix, please answer one final question.

♥ **What are some things you can do this next week to produce and grow in heavenly wisdom rather than in earthly wisdom?**

_____
_____

-- ♥ --

We give credit to human wisdom when we should give credit to the Divine guidance of God through childlike people who were foolish enough to trust God's wisdom and the supernatural equipment of God.
Oswald Chambers

God's secret wisdom comes with no diploma; we do not graduate from the "School of Godly Wisdom." It is a lifelong process.
Mimi Wilson
.

Your Thoughts

Questions

Comments

Prayer Requests

Prayer Answers

Week 5, Day 5

Peacemakers

Today's Focus: James 3:18; Matthew 5:9; Philippians 1:11; 4:6-7; Galatians 6:7-10; Hebrews 12:14; Romans 5:1; 12:18; John 14:27; Isaiah 26:3; Psalms 34:14

On the last day of this week we find James focusing on the person who is a peacemaker. He emphasizes that peacemakers will plant seeds of peace and reap a harvest of goodness (Jas. 3:18). For a minute think about those words—*planting seeds of peace and reaping a harvest of goodness.* How I yearn to be a peacemaker, but I fear at times I am just the opposite. Father, forgive me! Sometimes I seem to sow only seeds of discord. When that happens, the harvest is barren. Things are so difficult for me. I do the things I do not want to do; I say the things I do not want to say. I wonder whether anyone else has that problem. We both know, don't we? I do covet your prayers to be a seed-planter of peace; I will pray for you as well. Let's begin today's study about peacemakers by defining exactly what *peace* means.

According to the *Life Application Dictionary/Concordance, peace* means a calm repose, free of strife or discord, a harmony in personal relationships, and especially a right relationship with God. *Peacemakers* simply are people who sow peace. I feel almost peaceful just defining *peace;* the effect is very calming. Let's see what God's Word has to say.

♥ **Read Philippians 1:11. What does being filled with the** *fruit of salvation* **mean to you?**

_____

_____

The good things in our lives are produced by the Lord Jesus for us to bring glory and praise to our Heavenly Father. Therefore, if we are filled with the *fruit of our salvation,* we are filled with good things. The character traits produced within us flow from a right relationship with God. But what does this have to do with peace?

♥ **Read Romans 5:1. If you are in a right relationship with God, what do you have?**

_____

_____

Paul states that if we have been made right in God's sight by faith, then we have peace with God because of what Jesus our Lord has done for us. To have peace with our Heavenly Father means we have been made right with Him. It means we are reconciled with our God; no hostility exists between us, nor does any sin block our relationship with Him. Do we find any difference between the peace we have with God and having peaceful feelings? Certainly we do. Read on.

♥ **Read John 14:27. How does Jesus describe the peace He leaves you?**

_____

_____

♥ **Examine your life. Ask yourself whether you have the peace that only Jesus can give.**

_____

_____

Jesus says He leaves us with a gift—peace of mind and heart. The peace He gives isn't like the peace the world gives. Therefore, we are not to be troubled or afraid. Actually worldly peace is defined as the absence of conflict, whereas the peace that Jesus leaves us through the Holy Spirit is confident assurance in all circumstances and is a deep and lasting peace. With Jesus' peace we have no reason to fear the present or the future. What a difference!

♥ **Read Philippians 4:6-7. What instructions does this passage give about having true peace?**

_____

_____

Paul tells us we are not to worry about anything; instead, we are to pray about everything, to tell God exactly what we need, and to thank Him for all He has done for us. If we do this, then we will experience God's peace, which is far more wonderful than the human mind can understand. His peace will guard our hearts and minds as we live in Christ Jesus. Can you imagine never worrying about anything? Is this an impossibility? What about worries in our homes, on the job, and in other places?

Many years ago I was a chronic worrier. In fact my precious husband said to me, "Honey, I think you enjoy worrying. You seem to look for things to worry about." OUCH! Now that remark was like a big boulder that hit me very hard. Why? Because even though I did not want to hear those words, Archie spoke the truth. However, our Heavenly Father is so good! He showed me these two verses in Philippians; I had them embroidered and placed on the wall of our home. Since then, when I get the notion to start worrying, I refer back to those verses and reread them. Then an amazing thing happens after I pray and give the worry to my Father. Yep, you are right; the peace that passes all understanding just floods my soul. Now I am the person who prays about everything, from getting a parking space to keeping the electricity on while I am in an elevator to asking our Father to protect my family from all evil every day. God's peace is the only true peace; it springs from the assurance of knowing that our Heavenly Father is in control of everything.

♥ **Read Hebrews 12:14. We know we are to live in peace with our Heavenly Father, but with whom else are we to live in peace?**

Not only are we to live in peace with our Heavenly Father, we also are to live in peace with everyone else. Having a right relationship with God leads us to having a right relationship with fellow believers. To become more Christlike pursue peace with other believers whether you "feel" like doing so or not. I admit, sometimes I have to ask my Father to deal with some folks because I cannot do that on my own. But then I laugh and realize some folks probably have the same problem with me. Bottom line: live in peace with everyone (Rom. 12:18); work diligently at living in peace (Ps. 34:14). Things don't stop there; we are also to do good to everyone (Gal. 6:7-10), even our enemies!

♥ **Read Matthew 5:9. God has a promise for those who work for peace. How did you respond when you were reminded of His promise?**

According to the beatitudes God blesses those who work for peace. The Bible says *"they will be called the children of God."* Working for peace definitely is worth the effort.

♥ **Read Isaiah 26:3. After you read this verse, ask yourself if you have that *perfect peace* that God promises when you fix your thoughts on Him? If not, why not?**

Isaiah says if we trust in our Heavenly Father and keep our thoughts fixed on Him, then He will keep us in perfect peace. How awesome is that! We can have perfect peace even when chaos is all around us if we focus our minds on our Heavenly Father and His Word. Do you have that perfect peace—the peace that passes all understanding? If not, focus on HIM. Believe me, His perfect peace will flood your very soul! That's what is necessary to have a *faith that works*!

--♥ --

Whenever you obey God, His seal is always that of peace, the witness of an unfathomable peace, which is not natural, but the peace of Jesus. Whenever peace does not come, tarry till it does or find out the reason why it does not.

Oswald Chambers

Your Thoughts

Questions

Comments

Prayer Requests

Prayer Answers

Week 6
Characteristic 6:
Faith Produces Humility

Day 1
Waging War Within

Day 2
Infidelity and Unfaithfulness

Day 3
Resisting Makes Satan Flee

Day 4
Draw Close to God

Day 5
Criticizing and Condemning

Last week James spent a large amount of time contrasting earthly wisdom inspired by Satan with heavenly wisdom granted by God. In the first 12 verses of chapter 4, James stresses practical application for using heavenly wisdom effectively as we live day by day. Evidently James is the kind of person who is not afraid to confront evil. He must have realized a very important truth: *If evil is not challenged, it will not go away.* During this week we will focus on the strong pulls of worldliness and how these forces create conflicts within us that are harmful to our Christian growth of faith. Specific issues will be examined as we scrutinize the deadly results of their pursuit, such as quarrels and fighting, envy and covetousness, pride and arrogance, infidelity and unfaithfulness, and all <u>within</u> the body of believers. While studying the *Sixth Characteristic: Faith Produces Humility*, we will see James challenging us to humbly submit ourselves and draw near to our Heavenly Father to produce a new heart attitude within us as well as toward other people. Thanks for joining me as we embark on this next week's journey.

Heart Truths
Day 1: James 4:2
Day 2: James 4:4
Day 3: James 4:7
Day 4: James 4:8
Day 5: James 4:11

Week 6, Day 1

Waging War Within

† **Heart Truths:**

You want something but don't get it. You kill and covet, but you cannot have what you want. You quarrel and fight, You do not have, because you do not ask God
(Jas. 4:2 NIV).

Today's Focus: James 4:1-3; Matthew 5:21-22; 18:6; Titus 3:1-3; Mark 11:23-24; 1 John 3:15, 3:21-22; 5:14; Luke 18:1-8; John 14:13-14; Romans 7:14-25; Ephesians 4:31-32

Quarrels and fights, conflicts and disputes, battles with weapons, battles without weapons—whatever terminology you prefer to use—all of it is <u>wrong</u> when it happens within the body of believers. When these wars do occur, we are taken by surprise, because we may expect this type of behavior only from unbelievers rather than from our brothers and sisters in Christ. But realistically these behaviors actually happen much more within the body of believers than we would like to admit. WHY? Perhaps James asks the same question; obviously it was a huge problem during his day. Thankfully James is bold enough to address the problem. How I wish we had that same boldness today. Let's go to God's Word.

♥ **Read James 4:1-3. What questions does James ask?**

_____

_____

♥ **How does James respond to his own questions?**

_____

_____

♥ **How do you respond to these verses?**

_____

_____

♥ **Have you or a friend experienced destructive efforts from a fellow believer? If so, explain.**

_____

_____

My heart breaks to have to address the subject of *waging war within*, as this should never happen. However, you may know from either your own personal experience or perhaps from the experience of a friend that believers have a tendency to destroy their own people. Even James alludes to a murder which could be either a physical or a verbal assassination. Both cause deep, harmful pain, especially when the action springs from another believer. James asked two rhetorical questions: (1) *What is causing the quarrels and fighting among you?* (2) *Is not the cause your evil desires that wage war within your members?* James then answers his own questions by accusing the believers of lust, envy, jealousy, wrong motives, and selfish prayers, which all are motivated by wanting what you cannot have. James knows the believers no longer are sowing seeds of peace; instead they are at war with each other. This is sad, because a lot of innocent people get killed in any kind of war—and I do not necessarily mean physical death. Just think what something like this does to new believers who are caught in the crossfire or even unbelievers who may have shown an interest in trusting our Lord. Jesus says we are better off having a millstone tied around our necks and thrown into the sea than to cause one of these young ones to lose faith (Mt. 18:6). Dear Father, forgive us when the focus becomes ourselves and when *waging war within* becomes more important than does saving lost souls.

♥ **Read Matthew 5:21-22. How do you respond to Jesus' teachings in these verses?**

_____

_____

♥ **In what way can Jesus' teachings about anger and murder apply to your life?**

_____

_____

Jesus teaches not to become angry enough to murder, because if we do, we are guilty of committing murder in our hearts. Murder is a terrible sin and has its roots in anger and hatred. Thus anger also is a terrible sin, especially if it lashes out at another believer. It is a dangerous emotion that easily can get out of control and cause emotional hurt as well as spiritual damage. In First John we read, *Anyone who hates another Christian is really a murderer at heart. And you know that murderers don't have eternal life within them* (1 John 3:15). OUCH! Read further.

♥ **Read Titus 3:3. What does this verse say to you about evil desires and pleasures?**

_____

_____

According to Paul we are foolish and disobedient when we are slaves to our wicked desires and evil pleasures. When our lives became full of evil and envy, we hate others and they hate us. In other words we become a slave to evil desires when we disobey our Heavenly Father. Thus we see that hate and anger, envy and jealousy, pride and arrogance, as well as disobedience all lead to arguments and fighting within the body. How can this vicious cycle be stopped?

♥ **Read Romans 7:14-25. After you read these verses, think for a moment. Have you ever had a time in your life in which you had a similar experience such as the struggle Paul describes?**

_____

_____

Even the apostle Paul has the same kind of struggle that many of us face. He says he does not understand himself at all, for he really wants to do what is right, but he doesn't do it; instead, he does the very thing he hates. He admits he cannot help himself, because the sin inside of him makes him do evil things. He says he is rotten through and through regarding his old sinful nature. He really struggles with doing what is right; inevitably he does what is wrong instead. Sound familiar? Can you relate? I surely can. As he shares his frustration with us, we can learn that knowledge is not the answer, since Paul is very knowledgeable. We can learn that self-determination doesn't help us succeed, since Paul is very determined. We can learn that becoming a Christian does not remove all of our sin natures, since we will have temptations daily in our lives. Yet Paul realizes he needs help. The answer to his cry for help is in Jesus, our Lord. Paul's inward struggle is real; so is our struggle real for us, too. But like Paul we also need help. Rely on the power of Jesus to lift you up to victory over your sinful nature so that you no longer will be a slave to sin. However, if we lose the battle and fulfill our evil desires, we become competitors rather than brothers and sisters in Jesus. Let me explain.

In the past I worked in areas in which some people viewed me as a competitor rather than a colleague. One believer even tried to assassinate my character; this hurt deeply. Sometimes when people feel threatened, they battle for power and prestige, but as believers we are not to divide our loyalty between God and the world. Thus when incorrect assumptions are made, the conflict becomes a difficult matter with which to deal. My heart's desire is always to complement other health-care professionals and to build collegial relationships. I never want to be viewed as a competitor, because competition drives people to shameful actions and thoughts and decreases their ability to pray correctly.

Have you ever been the target of a sniper with well-aimed criticisms or the object of propaganda in which gossip is used to spread damaging information about you? Have you ever been involved in attacks from church members or in an ambush or had someone use you to get damaging information about others? No one is immune to being hurt. Beware that you are not the victim or the perpetrator.

♥ Read again James 4:2-3. How do you relate to what James is saying about prayer?

_____

_____

James says we have not because we ask not. When we ask, we do not receive because we ask with the wrong motives. These verses identify the three most common problems related to prayer: not asking, asking for wrong things, and asking for wrong reasons. Prayer is our lifeline! Allow our Heavenly Father to change your desires so you can communicate according to His will. Do we possibly not include God in our desires? We are told if we obey and do what pleases God, we can ask for anything (1 John 3:21-22 and Mark 11:23-24). We also are told to ask in accordance with His will (1 John 5:14); to ask in Jesus' name (John 14:13-14); and to be persistent in prayer (Luke 18:1-8). But the important thing is that we are to always ask for the right things with the right reasons. What about you? Are you asking in accordance with God's will for your life?

♥ Read Titus 3:1-2. What is Paul telling you to do as a believer?

_____

_____

♥ Read Ephesians 4:31-32. In these verses what is Paul's advice?

_____

_____

A light may be at the end of the tunnel. In Titus Paul tells us we are to be obedient, do what is good, not speak evil of anyone, avoid quarreling, be gentle, and show true humility to everyone. In Ephesians Paul instructs us to get rid of all bitterness, rage, anger, harsh words, slander, and malicious behavior; instead be kind to each other, tenderhearted, forgiving one another as God through Jesus forgives us. Could this be the cure for waging war within? To have a _faith that works_, be kind, tenderhearted, and forgiving toward each other. In other words treat others the way you want to be treated. Simple enough to say but difficult to do. What do you think?

--♥--

Be kind and compassionate to one another, forgiving each other, just as in Christ God forgave you

(Eph. 4:32 NIV).

Your Thoughts

Questions

Comments

Prayer Requests

Prayer Answers

Week 6, Day 2

Infidelity and Unfaithfulness

† **Heart Truths:**

Adulterers and adulter-esses! Do you not know that friendship with the world is enmi-ty with God? Whoever therefore wants to be a friend of the world makes himself an enemy of God (Jas. 4:4 NKJ).

Today's Focus: James 4:4-6; Ezekiel 16:5-19, 32; Jeremiah 3:20; Galatians 5:16-26; Romans 6:6-8; 8:5-8; Proverbs 3:34; 16:18-19; Matthew 6:24; John 15:18-21; 17:14; 1 Corinthians 6:19-20; 1 Peter 5:5-6; 1 John 2:15-17

Yesterday we studied about the damage that can be caused when believers quarrel and fight with each other. We know that when the church becomes a battleground, all effectiveness is lost; innocent people are hurt and deeply wounded. Believers who have personal conflicts with other believers hurt many people and not just the two people personally involved in the dispute. In today's study James identifies further proof of demonic wisdom. In fact James uses much harsher words when he calls believers *adulterers and adulteresses* to vividly describe spiritual infidelity and unfaithfulness. Let's open up our minds and hearts as we look into God's Word and try to understand and relate to what James is discussing.

♥ **Read James 4:4-6. Why do you think James called believers *adulterers*?**

_____

_____

In the Old Testament God refers to the people of Israel as *adulterers* because they try to combine their worship of God with the worship of idols such as Baal. Also Israel is compared many times to an *adulterous wife* who wants her husband yet also wants lovers. Thus James refers to believers as *adulterers* because they are trying to love God and have an affair with the world at the same time. Is this happening today? Of course it is! We as believers are inundated with the message to compromise. We are told that we need to "broaden our minds", be flexible, be more tolerant, and be "politically correct". Excuse me! Let's re-look at these worldly expectations. As believers why tolerate sin? Why excuse foul, nasty language? Why accept homosexuality as "normal"? Why excuse our young people sleeping together before marriage to see if they are "compatible"? Why watch a couple have sex in a movie theater or on a television set or on a computer? Why tolerate pornographic magazines and/or videos? I could go on and on. What a lot of nonsense! Sin is sin, whichever way you choose to coat it, when it directly opposes the teachings found in God's Word.

♥ Read Ezekiel 16:5-19, 32 and Jeremiah 3:20. How do you respond to the imagery that the Lord uses through Ezekiel?

_____

_____

These verses reflect the imagery of an unfaithful wife who turns away from the love of her husband and seeks other lovers. However, it is much more than that. It is the picture of a young baby whom God saves the day she is born and raises her from being a castaway to great glory as His bride. This is a picture of spiritual adultery because she turns from trusting the one and only true God to prostituting herself. This is Israel's story, but it also is ours. How? Because Israel adopts the customs of unbelievers and seeks alliances with heathen nations. She pushes God away for career, family, education, and pleasure. Have you ever done that? Maybe not overtly, but what about covertly? We don't have to learn through devastating experiences and the destructive results that sin produces. We have God's Word to show us how to live. Why not use it?

♥ Read Galatians 5:16-26. In these verses what two forces are being described?

_____

_____

♥ What are some experiences you have had in your life as you have struggled with these two forces?

_____

_____

Paul is describing two forces fighting within us: the power of the Holy Spirit and our old sin natures. He says the choices we make as believers never are free from this conflict. The old sin nature loves to do evil and is just the opposite from what the Holy Spirit wants for us. As you know, we all have evil desires with which we deal daily. Sometimes we deal with them minute by minute! But to effectively overcome these desires, draw on the power of the Holy Spirit.

♥ Read Romans 8:5-8. What do you experience if you allow the Holy Spirit to control your sinful nature?

_____

_____

How I praise God for my Savior and Lord, Jesus! If He had not offered me a way out, I would have been swallowed up in my sin. Once we say _yes_ to Jesus, we will experience life and peace through the Holy Spirit, who will control our minds if we let Him. This is a daily choice to consciously choose to center our life on our Heavenly Father. We no longer are slaves to sin, for the power of sin died with Jesus on the cross and set us free to share in His new life (Rom. 6:6-8). Are you allowing the Holy Spirit to control your nature?

♥ **Read Matthew 6:24. In this verse what does Jesus say about two masters?**

_____

_____

♥ **Have you ever had an experience in which you believed you were serving two masters? If so, what happened?**

_____

_____

Jesus reminds us that no one can serve two masters: we will hate one and love the other or be devoted to one and despise the other. Our society is so materialistic. People spend most of their time collecting and storing up materialistic treasures. But remember the old saying that we "can't take it with us" when we die. ALL will be left behind. Don't fall into this trap. Instead commit to your Heavenly Father and store up spiritual treasures that will be in heaven waiting for you when you get there, such as those whom you may have had a small part in leading to Jesus. These spiritual treasures are accomplished only through acts of obedience to our Father.

♥ **Read John 15:18-21 and 17:14. What can you expect from the world when you choose to obey your Heavenly Father rather than your sinful nature?**

_____

_____

Jesus says that the world will hate us as it did Him because we no longer belong to the world. Why? The world hates us because we do not have the same values nor do we cooperate by joining in the world's sin. The world sees believers as _living accusations_ against the world's wickedness. We follow Jesus and not Satan.

♥ **Read 1 Corinthians 6:19-20. To whom does your body belong?**

_____

_____

When we become believers, the Holy Spirit enters our lives; our bodies belong to our Heavenly Father. We no longer have the right to do everything we want to do, especially to yield to a desire from our old sin nature. Our Heavenly Father purchases us with a great price. Because Jesus frees us from our sin, we are obligated to His service. Therefore we must not violate God's standards for living. We can have no union between God's temple and idols; we are the temple of the living God (1 Cor. 6:19). As a believer do everything in your power to avoid situations that would cause you to divide your devotion to your Heavenly Father.

♥ **Read Proverbs 16:18-19. How did you relate to the warning sign these verses give?**

_____

_____

♥ **As you examine your life in God's mirror, do you ever recall anyone accusing you of having a pride problem? If so, what did you do about it?**

_____

_____

These verses warn us that *pride goes before destruction and haughtiness before a fall.* They further state it is better to *live humbly with the poor than to share plunder with the proud.* Proud people do not see stumbling blocks, since these people believe they are above the shortcomings of ordinary people. Sometimes we are especially vulnerable to pride because we do not see it. Everyone else around us may be aware of our pride and haughtiness, but we seem to be oblivious to it. This is perhaps another of Satan's tricks. So how can we recognize pride and do something about it? Do we dare ask a trusted friend whether he or she sees pride and haughtiness in us? Maybe we should!

♥ **Read 1 Peter 5:5-6. In these verses what advice does Paul give you?**

_____

_____

Paul tells younger men and women to accept the authority of older men and women. He further says that both should serve each other in humility, because God has set himself against the proud and shows favor to the humble (Prov. 3:34). In other words, respect those who are older, listen to those who are younger, and be humble enough to learn from each other.

Could the cure for evil desires be humility? Could this be the reason James in verse 7 tells us to first humble ourselves before God and then to resist the devil? Perhaps pride makes us so selfish and self-centered that we must humbly subject ourselves before God first. God's Word says that *pride* leads to disgrace, arguments, punishment, and humiliation and ends in destruction, whereas, *humility* leads to wisdom and respect and ends in honor. If we allow the Holy Spirit to fill us, we will have a *faith that works.* We will be able to distinguish the world's ways from the ways of

our Heavenly Father. We no longer will be called *adulterers* and *unfaithful!*
Tomorrow we will discuss in much more detail how we can resist the devil so he
will flee from us. Meanwhile, sleep well as you remember that God loves you.

---♥ ---

*Stop loving this evil world and all that it offers you, for when you love
the world, you show that you do not have the love of the Father in you.
For the world offers only the lust for physical pleasure, the lust for
everything we see, and pride . . . But if you do the will of God, you
will live forever*

(1 John 2:15-17).

*The proud resist God: in their understanding they resist the truths of
God; in their will they resist the laws of God; in their passions they
resist the providence of God; therefore, no wonder that God resists
the proud.*

Matthew Henry

Your Thoughts

Questions

Comments

Prayer Requests

Prayer Answers

Week 6, Day 3

Resisting Makes Satan Flee

> † **Heart Truths:**
>
> *So humble yourselves before God. Resist the devil, and he will flee from you*
> (Jas. 4:7).

Today's Focus: James 4:7; Matthew 4:1-11; Luke 22:31; Job 1:6-12; 2 Corinthians 10:3-5; Ephesians 6:10-18; 1 Peter 5:5, 6-9; 1 John 4:4; Revelation 12:10-12; 20:2

For the past two days we have studied about waging war within the body of believers and being unfaithful in the calling to our Heavenly Father. We realized that evil desires are inspired by Satan; our hearts broke when we were referred to as *adulterers* and *adulteresses*. We know we have a choice in our behaviors and attitudes, but sometimes making the right choice is difficult as the battle rages every single day of our lives. Today we will identify ways of combating these evil forces and rejoice as Satan is conquered by the power of the Holy Spirit. So without further ado let's begin.

♥ **Read James 4:7. What does this verse instruct you to do?**

_____

_____

Actually James gives us two very important instructions: to humble ourselves and to resist Satan. We are told if we do these two things, Satan will run from us. Let's examine both of these instructions.

Yesterday we mentioned briefly that humility may be a cure for evil desires. Just what does being humble and having humility mean? *Bamford's Bible Dictionary* states *humble* means we are not to think more highly of ourselves than we should. *Easton's Bible Dictionary* defines *humility* as a prominent Christian grace which is well-pleasing to God. He further says that humility preserves the soul in tranquility, makes us patient under trials, and is the avenue to glory. Both Matthew Henry and Strong identify *humility* as submission to God. According to 1 Peter 5:5 the greatest promises are made to the humble. Easton states, "It is a great paradox in Christianity that it makes humility the avenue to glory." What a contrast! Through the years many people have associated humility with weakness, which evidently is far from the truth. It is just the opposite. So with that in mind, let's continue.

♥ **Read Matthew 4:1-11. How does Jesus resist the devil's temptations?**

_____

_____

132

The devil, called *Satan*, is constantly fighting against those who follow and obey God. He is always trying to get us to live his way rather than God's way. In Scripture he even goes after Jesus. However, Jesus combats him with Scripture verses and obedience to His Heavenly Father. When Jesus actually says to him, "Get out of here, Satan", that is when the devil leaves Him. I find that interesting. Does it take a command from us for him to leave? Let's see what happens to Peter and Job.

♥ **Read and compare Luke 22:31 with Job 1:6-12. What does Satan ask to do to Peter and Job?**

_____

_____

♥ **Have you ever felt as though you have been "sifted like wheat"? Please explain.**

_____

_____

Satan prowls around seeking to destroy believers who love and serve the Lord. He asks Jesus' permission to have *all of Peter and to sift him like wheat*. Satan wants to crush Peter because if he does not, Peter will be instrumental in leading many to a believing faith in Jesus. However, Jesus tries to warn and reassure Peter that when he repents, his faith will be renewed and he will become a strong leader. Now let's look at what happens to Job.

In Scripture, Satan, also called *the accuser*, appears before God actively searching for someone to attack. One of Satan's greatest desires is to cause people to hate and renounce God. He will try anything with his lies and deception. Job is a righteous man with whom God is very pleased. Even though understanding the entire matter is difficult, we know from the story that God gives Satan permission to test Job. Why? I can't answer that. But we do know we have an awesome example in God's Word of a righteous man who remains faithful to the God he loves. Does Satan seek to destroy believers today? Of course he does. However, God uses those times to build our character and allow us to express our faith to the world. I do know from experience God may not remove us from a problem or challenge or even pain, but He definitely will go through it with us if we ask Him. In time it makes us stronger and more usable.

From these two examples we see that Satan's plans are to cause believers to have doubt, discouragement, defeat, diversion, and delay. He wants us to suffer, be persecuted, and feel alone, weak, and helpless. So how do we resist these tactics and make him flee?

♥ **Read 1 Peter 5:6-9. What instructions do these verses give you in resisting Satan?**

_____

_____

♥ **Have you had to use any of these instructions to resist Satan? If so, which ones have helped you?**

_____

_____

To resist Satan, we are to be humble under the mighty power of God, give all our worries and cares to Him, be careful and on the alert for Satan, take a firm stand against him, be strong in our faith, and know we are not alone in this battle. Please realize you are especially vulnerable to Satan's attacks when you feel alone, weak, and helpless. Thus we must remember we need to seek out other believers for support, because we really do find safety in numbers. After all, to bind together in prayer and support each other is one of the benefits of being a part of the body of believers. Don't let anyone tell you that to conquer, you must divide. This is not scriptural; it is a tactic of Satan! We are not to forsake the gathering together of the saints for any reason.

♥ **Read Ephesians 6:10-18. What kind of armor are you to wear in your battle against Satan?**

_____

_____

To withstand the attacks of Satan, we must depend on the Lord's mighty power and put on ALL the armor of God. Stand firm and put on the belt of truth, the body armor of righteousness, the shoes of peace, the shield of faith, the helmet of salvation, and the sword of the Spirit, which is the Word of God. We must pray at all times, stay alert, and be persistent. We are human; be careful not to wage war with human plans and methods. Instead, we are to use God's weapons, not worldly weapons, to knock down Satan's strongholds (2 Cor. 10:3-5). With His weapons we break down every proud argument that keeps people from knowing our Heavenly Father as well as conquer their rebellious ideas and teach them to obey Jesus. These weapons knock down Satan's strongholds.

♥ **Read Revelation 12:10-12 and 20:2. What do these verses say to you about the final outcome of Satan?**

_____

_____

That's right! Satan has been defeated! He knows his time is limited. He is defeated by the blood of Jesus and by our testimonies. We know the rest of the story, but that does not excuse us from wearing the armor and being cautious and prepared. We must <u>resist</u> Satan for him to flee.

♥ **Read 1 John 4:4. What encouragement does this verse give you?**

_____

_____

Dear friend, becoming frightened by Satan's wickedness and even feeling overwhelmed by our problems is so easy. However, we are to be encouraged, because *"Greater is He that is in you than he that is in the world"* (1 John 4:4 NAS). Satan may be alive and well and stirring up trouble, but our Heavenly Father is stronger; He conquers ALL evil. Our Father has not left us helpless! He gives us the Holy Spirit to guide the battle plans, instructions, and weapons. To have a *faith that works* be in submission to your Heavenly Father and resist Satan. Resisting Satan gives us the assurance he will flee from us and that his defeat is imminent. Wow! Thank You, Father!

--♥ --

Thank You, my Father, for protecting and providing for us. You are awesome. Knowing that the battle is yours helps so much. Please forgive me for wanting to hold on to things too tightly for I know when I give them to you, you take care of everything. Thank you for the assurance that "greater is He that is in me than he that is in the world." May each of us always listen and obey Your Holy Word.

In Jesus' name, Amen

Your Thoughts

Questions

Comments

Prayer Requests

Prayer Answers

Week 6, Day 4

Draw Close to God

Today's Focus: James 4:8-10; Luke 15:11-32; 18:9-14; Psalms 51:7; Hebrews 9:12-14; 10:19-22; Romans 6:11; John 13:1-10; Philippians 2:5-11; Isaiah 1:16; 57:15b; Malachi 3:7; Zechariah 1:3

As you know, yesterday's study instructed us to humbly submit ourselves before God and to resist Satan with the Holy Spirit's power. Today's study, along with the remainder of the Book of James, begins a series of commands based on these two instructions. For us to have a *faith that works*, both submission to our Heavenly Father and resisting Satan are required. Let's see how James begins these commands.

♥ **Read James 4:8-10. How do you relate to the first command James gives you?**

_____

_____

♥ **How do you personally draw near to God?**

_____

_____

James begins by telling us to *draw near to God* and that *He will draw near* to us. James even gives us instructions on how we are to draw near to God. James tells us that we are to wash our hands and purify our hearts. To purify your heart, be willing to actually shed tears for the wrong things you have done, grieve and be sorrowful for your actions, and humbly submit yourself before God. If you are willing to do this, God promises to lift you up and give you honor. Are you willing to do this? Let's look further at what these instructions mean.

♥ **Read Hebrews 10:19-22. According to these verses how do you enter into the presence of a Holy God?**

_____

The only way we can enter into the presence of our Holy God is to be clean and have a pure heart. The Scripture says that we can boldly enter into the presence of God because of the blood of Jesus. Scripture tells us that when Jesus died on the cross, His death removed the curtain that separates us from God's presence. Now all believers may enter into God's presence at any time. However, do we have a special way that we can be clean both on the inside and on the outside to be accepted into His presence? Read further.

♥ Read Hebrews 9:12-14. Do you relate to Christ's blood purifying you?

_____

♥ If you do, then how do you relate?

_____
_____

Under the old system the blood of goats and bulls was necessary to cleanse people from ritual defilement. However, since Jesus shed His blood for us, our hearts are purified from the evil deeds (sins) that lead to death. This enables us to draw near and worship the living God. Hallelujah! Jesus was and is the perfect, final sacrifice for our sins. Rules and rituals have never been able to fully cleanse people's hearts. Only through the blood of Jesus can we have a clean conscience freed from sin's power. Jesus' sacrifice transforms our lives and hearts and makes us clean. He is our high priest who cleanses us from the inside. But what about our outside? Does it also need to be clean to draw near to a Holy God?

♥ Read John 13:1-10. Why do you think Jesus washes the disciples' feet?

_____
_____

From Scripture we know Jesus is a servant leader who models a servant role before His disciples. As is customary in Jesus' day, servants wash people's feet as guests enter a home and especially before a meal. Therefore, Jesus takes this role on Himself and finishes cleansing the disciples by washing their feet. By doing this He shows the extent of His love and also demonstrates to them that they also are to serve each other as they take the message of salvation to a lost world. When we read these verses, we recognize that even though we may have bathed, Jesus totally cleanses us both on the outside and inside. How? Because when we are clean on the inside, this shows on the outside by our actions in what we say and do.

♥ Read Philippians 2:5-11. What characteristics of Jesus do you want to imitate?

_____
_____

If we humble ourselves, we will be exalted; greatness springs from serving. Wow!

What a paradox! As a believer, have the attitude of a servant; set aside your rights so you may serve others. Does this mean you are to develop an attitude of humility? If so, how do you do that?

♥ **Read Psalms 51:7 and Isaiah 1:16. As you read these two verses, describe how you think they <u>differ</u>.**

_____

_____

♥ **Can you describe a time in which you failed to recognize one of your sins?**

_____

_____

David is asking God to wash and purify him of his sins so he will be clean and whiter than snow, whereas God is instructing the people of the kingdom of Judah to wash their own selves to be clean so He no longer will see their evil deeds. Since both verses have to do with cleanliness, why do we see a difference with who does the washing? Could this have something to do with attitude? I think so. David recognizes his sins, whereas the people of Judah fail to recognize their sins. Have you ever been guilty of not recognizing your sins? I sure have.

♥ **Read Romans 6:11. How can you live for the glory of God?**

_____

_____

The only way we can live for the glory of God is to consider ourselves *dead to sin*. What does that mean? To me being *dead to sin* means to regard our old sinful nature as being unresponsive to sin. In other words, we are no longer to pursue our old, evil desires; instead, our desires are to live for the glory of our Heavenly Father. To me this sounds like an attitude change and maybe even a choice.

♥ **Read Malachi 3:7 and Zechariah 1:3. As you read these verses, what do you think they tell you to do?**

_____

_____

According to these verses our Heavenly Father promises us that if we return to Him, He will return to us. How awesome is that! Our Heavenly Father is so patient with us even when we disobey. He is always ready to accept us if we are willing to return to Him. A good example is the parable of the lost son who squanders his inheritance (Luke 15:11-32). We observe a father who patiently watches for his son to return home. The father, representative of our Heavenly Father, is delighted and filled with love that his son has returned; he immediately forgives his son and totally welcomes him back home. That is exactly what our Heavenly Father does for us. He only wants us to return to Him if we have gone astray. Do you need to return? If so, this is how you do it . . ..

♥ Read Isaiah 57:15b. What do you need to do if you have a broken relationship with your Heavenly Father?

_____

Our Heavenly Father wants us to repent and have changed hearts and attitudes if we have sinned and the relationship with Him has been broken. God's Word tells us if we repent, He will refresh us and give us new courage. When we look at the parable of the two men who pray, we know the tax collector is the one whose prayer God accepts (Luke 18:9-14). Why? Our Heavenly Father desires for you to have a repentant heart and attitude and not have a spirit of self-righteousness like that of the Pharisee. Self-righteousness leads to pride, causes hatred, and keeps us from learning anything from God.

To draw near to God and have Him draw near to you, be clean on the inside and outside through the blood of Jesus, be truly sorry and repent for the evil things you have done, and willingly return to your Heavenly Father with a humble spirit. If we do these things, God promises us that if our hearts are pure, we will move forward and will become stronger and stronger because our Heavenly Father will restore us. So, to have a _faith that works_, draw near to God. Have you drawn near to God and experienced His drawing near to you? Nothing compares to His Holy presence!

---♥---
The presence of God in a believer's life makes everything spiritual.
Mimi Wilson

Your Thoughts

Questions

Comments

Prayer Requests

Prayer Answers

Week 6, Day 5

Criticizing and Condemning

† Heart Truths:

Do not speak [evil] against one another brethren. He who speaks against a brother, or judges his brother, speaks against the law, and judges the law; but if you judge the law, you are not a doer of the law, but a judge of it (Jas. 4:11 NAS).

Today's Focus: James 4:11-12; Matthew 7:1-5, 12; 16:27; 22:37-39; Acts 11:2-18; Galatians 5:14-15; 1 Peter 2:1; John 8:7; 1 Corinthians 4:5; 2 Corinthians 12:20; Romans 14:10; 14:4, 10-13; Numbers 12:1-10; 2 Samuel 12:5-6; 2 Kings 2:22b-24

I'm always amazed to see how God's Word unfolds. We have just finished studying about our heart attitudes toward our Heavenly Father. Now James focuses on our attitudes and relationships with other believers. Does this sequence remind you of anything? The two greatest commandments—to love the Lord your God with all your heart, soul, mind, and strength and to love your neighbor as yourself (Mt. 22:37-39)—spring to my mind. We are told to love God by humbly submitting to Him and to love our brethren by not speaking evil against them. Let's see what *speaking evil* means.

♥ **Read James 4:11-12. What do you think** *speaking evil against against another person* **means?**

_____

_____

The Greek word for *to speak evil* is *katalaleite*. It refers to <u>any form</u> of speaking evil against another person. It can mean to slander or make false charges against someone, or it can mean to speak the truth in an unkind way. It can mean gossiping or spreading things that no one else should know. It can mean criticizing someone or that person's authority to make them look bad. It can mean backbiting, which would destroy any good they are doing. In other words *to speak evil* has the potential to do great harm. Ouch! Are you guilty? I know I am. All my life I have been plagued with a critical spirit; I really have to be on guard, because that is the exact area in which Satan attacks me. One thing I hopefully have learned through the years is to just keep my big mouth shut if I am tempted to speak evil about someone. Now, this is not easy, but at least that represents some improvement. One verse always occurs to me when I am tempted to speak evil. Let's read it together.

♥ **Read Matthew 7:12. What does this verse say to you?**

_____

If I can remember always to treat others as I would have others treat me, then at least half of the battle would be won about the temptation to speak evil.

♥ **Read Matthew 7:1-5. What does Jesus tell you to do about judging another?**

_____

_____

♥ **Have you ever had a problem about judging other people? If so what are some traits about another person that would bother you?**

_____

_____

Jesus commands us to stop judging others, or else we will be judged accordingly. Whatever measure we use to judge others, that measure also will be used to judge us. Jesus uses a very graphic illustration. He tells you to look in the mirror and remove the log out of your own eye before you try to get the speck out of your friend's eye. He even calls us *hypocrites*. Now that hurts! But as folks say, "If the shoe fits, wear it." I realize that what really bothers me the most about someone else is the trait I see in that person which reminds me of my own bad trait or behavior. Interesting! Perhaps before you criticize someone, check to see if you deserve the same criticism. Maybe if you judge yourself first, you may be more forgiving and loving toward other believers.

♥ **Read Galatians 5:14-15. Can you relate to what happens to you when you are not motivated to love others?**

_____

_____

According to Galatians if we do not love, we will always bite and devour each other. Maybe that is when we need to stop and perhaps make a list of that person's good qualities. My grandpa, Ben, always liked to believe everyone had some good in him or her. So maybe we need to make an effort to find this good point, which would be much better than criticizing and devouring.

♥ **Read 1 Peter 2:1. What does Peter say you are to get rid of?**

_____

_____

Peter tells us to rid ourselves of all malicious behavior and deceit including hypocrisy, jealousy, and backstabbing. Even Paul is concerned that he might find quarreling, jealousy, outbursts of anger, selfishness, backstabbing, gossip, conceit, and disorderly behavior in the lives of the believers in Corinth (2 Cor. 12:20). Paul fears that the evil culture of Corinth has influenced the believers negatively. These behaviors are still very much a problem today. Let's live differently than unbelievers and not let these horrible things influence our own behavior.

♥ **Read Romans 14:4, 10-13. What are you warned not to do?**

_____

_____

These verses warn us we are not to condemn anyone, because each of us is accountable and responsible to Jesus. But what does *condemning someone* mean? To *condemn someone* is to declare that person guilty and literally to pass a sentence on that person. How awful! I cannot answer for you, but I surely do not want to be guilty of condemning anyone. That is only our Heavenly Father's job; for that I am very grateful. Let's look at the following example.

♥ **Read John 8:7. What happens to the adulterous woman?**

_____

_____

The entire account of the adulterous woman is found in John 8:1-8; however, for now I want to focus only on the significance of Jesus' statement, "*Let those who have never sinned throw the first stone.*" Jesus upholds the penalty of the law, yet, He changes the focus by saying only a person <u>without sin</u> could throw the first stone. By doing this, He emphasizes the importance of compassion and forgiveness. Sometimes we are too quick to judge others. We do not stop to evaluate the consequences. Let's look at a couple of examples.

♥ **Read Numbers 12:1-10. What happens to Miriam when she criticizes Moses for having a Cushite wife?**

_____

♥ **Read 2 Kings 2:22b-24. What happens to the boys who mock Elisha and laugh at his baldness?**

_____

God's Word has many examples of how people pay a penalty for their critical spirits, but for now we will look at only two examples. When Miriam criticizes Moses, she is stricken with leprosy. When the group of boys mock Elisha, they are killed by bears. Sometimes criticism may not focus on the real issue, such as in the case of Miriam. Her real issue is a growing jealousy of Moses' position and influence. Rather than admit she has a problem with envy and pride, she seeks to create a distraction from the real issue. The boys are not merely teasing Elisha about his baldness, they are being very disrespectful of God's messenger. Sometimes people try to magnify others' traits yet try to excuse their own. Look for a moment at David's reaction to the story the prophet Nathan tells him (2 Sam. 12:5-6). David is furious at the person in the story, yet he does not realize Nathan is talking about him. Often we condemn in others our own character flaws. Ask your Heavenly Father to help you understand and see your own flaws more clearly. That means bringing out God's mirror again to look within ourselves.

♥ **Read Matthew 16:27 and 1 Corinthians 4:5. After reading these verses how did you respond to who is responsible for judging others?**

_____

According to God's Word only Jesus has the authority for judging the deeds of people. Someday we will all stand before the judgment seat of God (Rom. 14:10) as each of us is accountable to Jesus. However, only our Heavenly Father can know a person's heart; only He is capable of judging that person's salvation. God's Word warns us not to be quick to judge (Acts 11:2-18), because we may not have heard the <u>whole</u> story! Maybe the Holy Spirit is trying to teach us something. To have a *faith that works*, avoid speaking evil against anyone or being quick to judge.

---♥ ---

Backsliding starts when knee bending stops.
Skip Heitzig

Backstabbing starts where knee bending stops.
Anne's version

Your Thoughts

Questions

Comments

Prayer Requests

Prayer Answers

Week 7
Characteristic 7:
Faith Produces Trust in God

Day 1
Uncertainty of Tomorrow

Day 2
If the Lord Wills

Day 3
Not Doing Right . . . a Sin?

Day 4
Warnings to the Rich

Day 5
Cheating Others

As we progress into the last chapter of James, I realize we have only three more weeks; then our time together will be concluded. I don't know about you, but for me this has been quite a journey which almost can be compared to a roller-coaster ride. At times I have felt vulnerable; the tears have flowed as we covered certain topics. With other topics I have felt a sense of security and peace as though I was all wrapped up in the blanket of my Heavenly Father's love. What about you? Have you experienced any of these feelings? James has much to offer believers about how to achieve a *faith that works*. This week we will focus on the seventh and final *Characteristic of Faith: Faith Produces Trust in God*. We will find ourselves digging deeply into the last five verses of chapter 4 as well as the first six verses of chapter 5. Hopefully after you complete these 11 verses, you will develop an even deeper trust in your Heavenly Father, because that's His desire for you. So bend your knees in prayer, get into your favorite comfy chair, open your sword, which is the Word of God, and let's begin!

Heart Truths
Day 1: James 4:14
Day 2: James 4:15
Day 3: James 4:17
Day 4: James 5:3
Day 5: James 5:4

Week 7, Day 1

Uncertainty of Tomorrow

Today's Focus: James 4:13-14; Proverbs 27:1; Psalms 39:5; Luke 12:16-21; Acts 21:11-14; 1 Corinthians 6:19-20; Job 7:7; Romans 4:20-21

During these next three days, we will discover James persuading us to progress from humbly submitting ourselves to our Heavenly Father to entrusting everything we do to Him. Life is a gift to appreciate and be thankful for every day. As believers let's entrust that gracious gift to the "Giver of Life," our Holy Sovereign God, who is in control. Our Heavenly Father does not make mistakes, as He made each of us for a purpose. Today's study reminds us that sometimes we make our plans without ever consulting God in them. Let's see what God's Word has to say.

♥ **Read James 4:13-14 and Proverbs 27:1. How do you relate to the warnings these verses give you?**

_____

_____

James warns us about being overly confident in our plans for the day as well as our plans for the future. He reminds us that we make specific plans for certain days without ever considering God in those plans. He says we make those plans without ever knowing what tomorrow will bring. James further reminds us that life is like a morning fog that is here for a little while and then is gone. In Proverbs, Solomon tells us not to brag about tomorrow, since we do not know what the day will bring. How depressing! But how true. For years I hung a cross-stitch on my wall that simply said, "Life is Fragile, Handle with Prayer." Those simple words were a constant reminder that whatever plans I may make, I must pray <u>first</u> to see if that is what my Heavenly Father wants for me. I could share with you many stories about things that happened to me before I learned this valuable lesson. Instead let's see in what other ways the Bible refers to *life*.

♥ **Read Job 7:7 and Psalms 39:5. As you read these verses, to what is your life compared?**

_____

_____

Both verses refer to *life* as being a breath. One verse even compares life to the width of our hand. Let's think for a moment; what is a breath really like? Breathing is automatic; unless we are having a physical problem, we rarely think about it. However, when you think of breathing in and breathing out, you realize a few seconds are necessary for each breath. Now look at your hand; how wide is your hand? Not very wide, is it? We realize our lives here on earth are very short compared to eternity. So how can we make the most of the life that our Father has given us? How do we deal with all the uncertainties that life brings?

♥ **Read Luke 12:16-21. In this parable what truth does Jesus emphasize?**

_____

_____

♥ **Have you ever had a time in your life in which, after your plans fell through, you realized this was because you did not consult God first? Please explain.**

_____

_____

In these verses Jesus tells us about the parable of the rich fool. Jesus emphasizes that the man dies before he can use all he has stored up in his barns. Why? Evidently the man is taking care only of himself with no regard or concern for any-one else. Jesus calls a person a *fool* who stores up earthly wealth and does not have a rich relationship with God. The old saying, "You can't take it with you", certainly is true. But these verses mean even more than that. Jesus is reminding us that life is brief; if we leave our Heavenly Father out of our plans, we will not succeed. Do you include God in your plans? Think about it.

♥ **What are some ways you might leave God out of your plans?**

_____

_____

What ways sprang to your mind? Here are some possible ways that we leave God out of our plans. Have any of these applied to you?

We leave our Heavenly Father out of our plans when we—
• see our work as a way to make money to get what we want;
• define our money as our optimum objective and an end to our means;
• think that we are in control rather than allowing God to be;
• without prayer make practical decisions about career, moving, education, choosing a life partner, spending money, retirement, and so forth;
• convince ourselves that God is not interested in or is too busy for the "small" matters of our lives.

I admit that in the past, some of these ways have applied to me. What about you? I pray not, but if so, what can be done to correct it?

♥ Read 1 Corinthians 6:19-20. To whom do you belong?

_____

Precious folks, we do not belong only to ourselves; God purchased us with a high price! Therefore, honor God with your entire being. We belong to God; His purpose for our lives must take precedence over our own selfish desires. Jesus' death may free us from sin, but it also obligates us to His service. Think for a moment: if you were a visitor in a foreign country, you would not violate the laws of that country; neither are you to violate the standards God expects of you. Therefore, we cannot leave God out of our plans, especially when we deal with the uncertainties of this life.

♥ How do uncertainties affect you?

_____

_____

♥ Read Romans 4:20-21. How do uncertainties affect Abraham?

_____

_____

Uncertainties are things which may or may not happen. We cannot let them affect the trust we have in our Heavenly Father. In the Bible story Abraham never wavers in believing God's promise. He consistently trusts God, because he is convinced God will fulfill His promises. Abraham is strengthened through the uncertainties he faces in his life and is an example of faith in action. Read further.

♥ Read Acts 21:11-14. How does Paul react to uncertainties?

_____

_____

We do not have to let uncertainties affect our plans if we know those plans are made with the Lord. Paul is willing to obey God even when he knows he will be imprisoned in Jerusalem. If we really want to do God's will, we accept what accompanies that choice—even if pain is involved. What are you willing to do? Are you willing to make your Heavenly Father the key person in your plans? Actually we have no reason to make plans as though God does not exist, because the future is in His hands. However, in planning for the future be flexible enough to hold on loosely to those plans. Keep in mind, you may not know what the future holds, but we do know WHO holds the future. Whew, what a relief! What about you? A *faith that works* is a faith that completely trusts in our Heavenly Father with all of life's uncertainties, including what tomorrow will bring. Are you willing to let Him have all your uncertainties and all of your tomorrows? I hope so!

-- ♥ --

Realizing the future is uncertain not only teaches us trust in God, it also helps us properly value the present.

John Wesley

Your Thoughts

Questions

Comments

Prayer Requests

Prayer Answers

Week 7, Day 2

If the Lord Wills

Today's Focus: James 4:15-16; Acts 18:21; 1 Corinthians 5:6; Matthew 6:10, 33; Romans 12:2; John 6:38; Luke 22:42; Daniel 4:28-37; Hebrews 13:20-21

Inshallah! This is an Arabic term meaning "Lord Willing" and frequently is used about almost everything in the Middle East. For example, if I ask a taxi driver to take me somewhere, he usually responds with *"Inshallah."* If my husband and I ask our Muslim friends over for coffee or a visit, they also respond with *"Inshallah."* Actually, most requests and even many problems are responded to with the word *"Inshallah."* If an illness or an accident occurs, depending on the conversation, the response may be *"Inshallah."* After living in several Middle Eastern countries, I began wondering why my Muslim friends use this term so much and my Christian friends do not. Aren't we, as believers, also expected to respond with "Lord willing" about all of our plans? Now I admit I believe some of my Muslim friends take things to the extreme, even to the point of blaming God for all things, but where is the balance in how we see the will of our Heavenly Father? Let's look at what God's Word says.

♥ **Read James 4:15-16. What do these verses tell you to say about your plans?**

_____

_____

According to these verses, if we do not say "If the Lord wills" when we do this or that, we will be boasting about our own plans; such boasting is considered evil. Even Paul says "God willing" about the plans he makes to return to Antioch of Syria (Acts 18:21). Folks, have we missed the point here? Just how important is verbally saying, "Lord willing"? What happens if we do not say it? Could more be involved to this phrase than merely verbalizing the words "Lord willing"?

♥ **Read 1 Corinthians 5:6. What do you think happens when you boast and do not seek God's will on things?**

_____

_____

Paul warns us that if we boast about our spirituality, yet our actions do not reflect our words, then a big problem results. The Corinthian believers are boasting about their spirituality, yet they have allowed a blatant sin to affect the church. They had not even considered what would be God's will for them about how to correct the problem. James and Paul both say that "boasting is harmful." Look at the example of Nebuchadnezzar.

♥ Read Daniel 4:28-37. What happens to Nebuchadnezzar when he boasts of his accomplishments and leaves God out?

_____

_____

Nebuchadnezzar is driven from human society and even acquires some animal and bird-like characteristics. He eats grass like a cow, grows long hair like the feathers of an eagle, and his nails are like the claws of a bird. However, when he arrives at his senses, he gives praise, honor, and glory to the God of Heaven. God is sovereign and is above all kings, presidents, and authorities. He is also sovereign over all of our plans. God humiliates Nebuchadnezzar to demonstrate that He is the actual Lord of the nations. Never allow your accomplishments to cause you to forget your Heavenly Father. But what does saying "Lord willing" have to do with your plans and accomplishments?

♥ Read Matthew 6:33. What does this verse instruct you to do?

_____

_____

Jesus said if we make the *Kingdom of God* our primary concern, He will give us all we need from day to day. In other words, we are to put God first in every area of our lives. When you exchange your will for His will and your desires for His desires, you will see a big difference in your life. That is a promise from your Almighty Holy God. But how do you know His will?

♥ Read Romans 12:2. What change is necessary before we can know God's will?

_____

_____

In this verse we are told to let God transform us into new people by changing the way we think. Then we will know what God wants us to do; we will know how good and pleasing and perfect His will really is. The only way to be transformed into that new person is to allow the Holy Spirit to renew, reeducate, and redirect our minds. By the way this transformation at times can be quite painful. Much like a butterfly we go through a complete metamorphosis. We no longer are caterpillars crawling around in the dirt; we become butterflies who can soar with our Heavenly Father.

Several years ago, we acquired an old piano that needed total refurbishing. A Christian brother visited us to help us restore it. As usual our conversation began to focus on spiritual things. He asked me what my greatest desire in life was. Without hesitating for one moment, I blurted out, "To do God's will." Now actually, I was a bit taken back by my own response, but that response turned out to be the turning point in my life. From that day until now my Heavenly Father has been changing me into that butterfly to do His will. This is very painful at times, because He has had to really do a job on me. You see, I harbored a lot of hatred and anger in my life because of my past, but He removed it completely. I have become very transparent; God has used me to help many folks who have experienced some of the same things I once did. My personality has even mellowed through the years to the point that my Myers-Briggs personality test results totally changed from the first time I took it years earlier. How my Father has changed me is amazing and at times almost humorous. I praise the Lord for those changes. If you let God change you, you will know His will and what to do. Read on.

♥ **What are some ways you can know God's will for your life?**

_____

_____

We can know God's will through several ways. We can know God's will through—

• Scripture	2 Kings 23:2-3
• Prayers and fasting	Daniel 9:3-4
• Submission to the Holy Spirit	Isaiah 6:8
• Circumstances and counsel	Proverbs 24:6

I challenge you to look up each of the above verses and discover the ways for yourself. Through the years I have sought my Heavenly Father's will about numerous decisions and problems. My searching may have happened through hours of prayer on my knees, from fasting for long periods of time, from recognizing the circumstances and divine appointments He placed in my life, or through the counsel of godly friends. However, my experience has been that my Heavenly Father always seals His will for me through the Holy Scriptures. Now I am not saying that determining His will has to be done this exact way; I am only saying that this is how He reveals His will to me. So, how does He reveal His will to you?

♥ **Read Matthew 6:10. When Jesus teaches you about prayer, what does He say about God's will?**

_____

Evidently seeking the will of our Heavenly Father must be very important. Even Jesus emphasizes following God's will by placing the sentence, *"May Your will be done here on earth, just as it is in heaven"*, in the model prayer as He teaches us how to pray. In asking for God's will to be done, we are praying for His ultimate purpose to be accomplished. When Jesus agonizes in the garden before His arrest, He prays for God's will to be done rather than His own (Luke 22:42). Jesus must dread the upcoming trials, but He is committed to do what God wants Him to do. Are we committed to do what God wants us to do?

♥ **Read John 6:38. What do you think Jesus is sent to earth to do?**

_____

_____

Jesus tells us that He has been sent from heaven to do the will of His Heavenly Father who sent Him, not to do what He wants to do. Jesus' purpose on earth is to do the will of God. Isn't this a good purpose for us as well?

♥ **Read Hebrews 13:20-21. If you agree to do the will of God, what will He do for you?**

_____

_____

According to Scripture if we agree to do the will of our Father, He will equip us with all we need to accomplish His will. He also will produce in us, through the power of Jesus, all that is pleasing to Him. When we allow God to change us from within, He then will use us to help others. How awesome is that!

Are you considering God's will in all of your plans? If not, why not? He is the one and only sovereign God. He knows what is best for your life. To know and do the will of your Heavenly Father, recognize that God's will is higher than yours, submit your will to His will, and pray and listen as He tells you what to do. Doing these things produces a deeper trust in your Heavenly Father and enables you to have a *faith that works. Lord willing* or *Inshallah* are powerful expressions; never use them lightly. Let the desire spring from a sincere heart to really want to do His will. Believe me, you will not regret it!

---♥---

God not only expects me to do His will; but He is in me to do it.
                                                            Oswald Chambers

According to Max Lucado, we learn God's will by spending time
in His presence.

Your Thoughts

Questions

Comments

Prayer Requests

Prayer Answers

Week 7, Day 3

Not Doing Right . . . a Sin

Today's Focus: James 4:17; John 9:41; Leviticus 4:1-2; 5:1, 4; 10:1-2; 2 Peter 2:20-21; Numbers 31:14-16; Romans 13:10; Revelation 3:19

For the past two days we have studied about trusting everything we do to our Heavenly Father. We realize a *faith that works* completely trusts in God with all of the uncertainties that tomorrow brings. We also realize a *faith that works* recognizes God's will as being higher than ours and that He wants us willingly to submit to His will with everything we say and do. As believers we are never to leave God out of our plans. In today's lesson we will take one last glance at trusting everything we do to our Heavenly Father. Let's see what James has to say.

♥ **Read James 4:17. What do you think James means by this verse?**

_____

James seems to be adding up all the moral problems he addresses in the first four chapters of his book. He is saying that since you know what to do, then simply do it, because if you do not, it is a sin. What do you think he means by this statement? Sometimes as human beings we think only doing something wrong is a sin. But it goes deeper than that. James is saying that not doing what is right also is a sin. How can that be? Let me ask you a few questions. Do you sin if you know the truth about something and refuse to tell it? Do you sin if you avoid someone who you know needs your help? Do you sin if you refuse to visit that neighbor who needs your friendship? Do you sin if you ignore people and instead make excuses for your busy-ness? Do you sin if you isolate yourself when Jesus expects you to serve others? I cannot answer those questions for you, but again we are back to the old saying, "If the shoe fits, wear it." I seem to have a lot of shoes to put on! What about you?

♥ **Read John 9:41. What is your response to Jesus' teaching in this verse?**

_____

_____

Jesus is teaching about spiritual blindness rather than physical blindness. He says if we truly are blind, we won't be guilty, but we remain guilty because we claim we can see. Jesus tells the Pharisees that because of their spiritual blindness they have no excuse; they claim they can see. In other words their sins of stubbornness and self-satisfaction have blinded them from knowing the real truth. The longer we walk with Jesus, the more we get to know Him. As we walk with Him, our eyes are opened; we learn His truths. He is the one who gives us spiritual insight and understanding. Therefore, when we know the truth, we are responsible for acting on that truth.

♥ **Read Leviticus 4:1-2. What does God say about unintentional sins?**

_____

_____

♥ **In reflecting over your life, what unintentional sins have you committed?**

_____

_____

The Lord through Moses gives the Israelites specific instructions on how to deal with unintentional sins. _Unintentional sins_ are sins that are done without realizing until much later that they are sins. Even though they are not intentional, that does not make them any less sinful. Our Heavenly Father wants us to be aware of all sins so we can be forgiven for them. Since the law is given to teach and guide people, let's look at a couple of these "unintentional sins".

♥ **What "unintentional sins" do the following verses mention?**

Leviticus 5:1

_____

Leviticus 5:4

_____

In verse one we are held responsible for testifying about something we have witnessed. If we refuse to testify, we are subject to punishment. In verse four we are warned to avoid making rash vows, because we are held responsible for fulfilling them. Did I hear you say, "How does that apply to me"? Let me ask you something. Have you ever promised to do something and then realized you made that promise foolishly? As a believer keep your word, even if you make a promise too tough to keep—unless, of course, that promise leads to sin.

Several years ago I signed a three-year contract to serve as the director of a nursing program at a religiously affiliated college. The first year was very stressful getting adjusted, evaluating the program, and identifying the barriers and bridges. The second year intensified, problems escalated, and so many negative things happened that I had to stay on my knees to survive. Many times I just wanted to throw my hands up in the air and leave. But I had made a commitment. I firmly believed I had to remain until my Heavenly Father told me to move on. As painful as it was, in retrospect, that was one of the most difficult yet "character-building" times of my entire life. Had I left, would it have been an "unintentional sin"? I think it would have. A promise is a commitment. Be careful of the ones you make.

♥ **Read 2 Peter 2:20-21. To what do you think Peter refers in this verse?**

_____

_____

Peter speaks about people who have learned about how to be saved through Jesus but who reject the truth. He says people would be better off having never known the right way to live than to know it and then reject it. We are responsible for what we know and learn. We are responsible for our attitudes. Read on.

♥ **Read Numbers 31:14-16. Why do you think Moses is so furious with the military commanders who return from battle?**

_____

_____

God commands Israel to destroy the Midianites because they are enticing Israel into Baal worship. Instead Israel takes the women as captives. Moses immediately deals with their sin—the same thing we are to do when we discover we have sin in our lives. Later we find that when the Israelites enter into the Promised Land, their attitude of indifference to sin eventually ruins them. An indifferent attitude will destroy! Look at what happens to Aaron's sons, Nadab and Abihu. They are primary candidates to become high priest; however, they treat lightly the direct commands of God. They burn a different kind of fire before the Lord than what God has commanded. So fire blazes forth from the Lord's presence and burns them up; they die there before the Lord (Lev. 10:1-2). Their indifference causes their death.

♥ **Read Revelation 3:19. How do you relate to the instruction God gives to the church at Laodicea?**

_____

_____

♥ **Have you ever had a problem with indifference? Explain.**

_____

_____

156

God tells this lukewarm church to be diligent and turn from its indifference. God tells us, too, to be diligent and turn from our indifference. Our Heavenly Father wants us to return to Him. Sin we commit out of ignorance or indifference deserves punishment. However, God desires for us to have a close relationship with Him and provides a way for us if we will confess our sins, serve Him, worship Him, and study His Word. The Holy Spirit can give us just the spark of love we need if we are willing to do as He directs.

♥ **Read Romans 13:10. What satisfies God's requirements?**

_____

_____

This verse says love satisfies all of God's requirements and does no wrong to anyone. We tend to rationalize and excuse our indifference toward other people to justify our actions. However, Jesus does not leave any loopholes in the law when He says to love God and to love your neighbor as yourself. Love demands we go beyond legal requirements and imitate Jesus, who saves our souls. So to have a *faith that works*, trust everything to your Heavenly Father and act on those things you know to be true. Maybe we need to restore a broken relationship or do a kind deed to help someone. What do you know you need to do? Then go do it!

---♥ ---
Never allow a truth of God that is brought home to your soul to pass without acting on it, not necessarily physically, but in will.
Oswald Chambers

Your Thoughts

Questions

Comments

Prayer Requests

Prayer Answers

Week 7, Day 4

Warnings to the Rich

Today's Focus: James 1:9-11; 2:2-4; 4:4-5; 5:1-3; Luke 12:15, 33; Romans 12:1-2; Ephesians 5:5; 1 Timothy 6:7-11, 17-19; Proverbs 11:4, 28; Ecclesiastes 2:18; Mark 9:43; 10:17-31; Matthew 6:19-21; 16:26; 19:21-22; Isaiah 5:8-9; Revelation 18:4-8

After studying the first four chapters of James you probably have noticed the frequent warnings he gives to those who possess riches. In chapter one James warns us against the arrogance of riches; in chapter two he warns us against partiality based on wealth; and in chapter four he warns us against being seduced by the world. Now in chapter five James warns us about the worthlessness of riches. He is showing us what riches can do to people as well as to those associated with them. James proclaims that riches can lead to greed, self-sufficiency, destruction, and judgment. Please realize James is not saying rich people are worthless; instead, he is saying the love of money and riches will destroy us. As you know, we all need money to live. Churches need money to proclaim the gospel; so do Christian leaders and missionaries. In these next two days listen carefully as we discover exactly what James warns us about.

♥ Read Mark 9:43. How can you respond to what Jesus is saying in this verse?

_____

_____

Jesus says if your hand causes you to sin, cut it off. You are better off entering heaven with only one hand than to go into hell with two hands. Jesus warns that the choices we make have eternal consequences and that we need to be mindful of the temptations that can destroy us. But what does this have to do with riches? If your ultimate goal in life is to be wealthy, examine your true motives to see if they are in line with God's desires for you. If not you can become so enticed and enslaved to acquiring wealth that you are in danger of forgetting God (Mark 10:23). We also are in danger of taking advantage of others (Isa. 5:8-9), becoming greedy (Eph. 5:5), and turning into self-sufficient people (Rev. 18:4-8).

♥ Read 1 Timothy 6:9-10. What does Paul say will happen to you if your focus in life becomes an obsession to be rich?

_____

_____

In 1 Timothy, Paul warns that people who long for riches fall into temptation and become trapped by many foolish, harmful desires that plunge them into ruin and destruction. Since the "love of money" is the root of all kinds of evil, some people who crave money wander from the faith and bring many sorrows on themselves. It becomes an endless cycle—the more we have, the more we want. Beware of becoming part of that cycle, as it can end in destruction as it did for a dear friend of ours.

When we first met our friend whom we will call Bill, he appeared to be an humble, God-fearing man who loved the Lord. He had a sweet, beautiful wife and precious children. Bill was very intelligent and seemed to possess volumes of amazingly good judgment in business transactions. You might say Bill had the "Midas touch"; everything in which he took part was successful. People sought him out for advice; Bill became the CEO of a large corporation. He used millions of dollars to acquire and sell other corporations like I would use a few coins to buy and sell clothes. But something happened to Bill: he started getting self-sufficient and greedy. Many people who trusted Bill were hurt, as his greed and self-sufficiency consumed him. Finally Bill lost everything: his family and his fortune. Only our Heavenly Father knows what else he lost. We have witnessed Bill go from being on top of the world to being led off in handcuffs. Please join me as we continue to pray for Bill and his family.

♥ Read James 5:1-3. How do you respond to how James describes riches?

_____

_____

James vividly describes the worthlessness of accumulating wealth, fine clothes, gold, and silver. He emphasizes that storing up earthly treasures here on earth are futile; they cannot be taken with us. Even Solomon says he is disgusted that he must leave the fruit of his diligent work behind for others to enjoy (Eccl. 2:18). God's Word shows that diligent work bears no lasting fruit if you work only to earn money and to gain possessions. At your death <u>everything</u> will be left behind!

♥ Read Matthew 6:19-21 and Luke 12:33-34. In these verses what does Jesus say about storing up earthly treasures?

_____

_____

In Jesus' teaching about money He explicitly tells us <u>not</u> to store up treasures on earth, where they can be eaten by moths and get rusty and where thieves can steal them. Instead we are to store up treasures in heaven, where they never will be moth-eaten or rusty or stolen. In Luke, Jesus says to sell what we have and give to those in need; this will store up treasure for us in heaven! Jesus reminds us that where our treasure is, our hearts and thoughts will be there also. He further emphasizes that our souls and eternal destinies are much more important is than gaining the materialism of the whole world (Mt. 16:26). What about your treasures? Do you need to make any changes in your life?

♥ Read Romans 12:1-2. What benefits do you receive from allowing God to change you?

_____

_____

When we allow God to transform and change us, this gives us the strength to refuse conformity to this world's values. If we are wise, we will decide that worldly behavior is off limits. Therefore, choose godly standards over earthly standards. Why? Riches and money cannot buy us salvation (Prov. 11:4), nor can money ever satisfy us (Luke 12:15). Real life is not measured by what we have. No amount of riches can ever buy reconciliation with God. He wants only your love and obedience. Trust in your Heavenly Father and not in money or riches. The "good" life has absolutely nothing to do with riches. Of course that is the exact opposite of what you hear from advertisers on a daily basis. Millions of dollars are spent every year to entice us to buy more and more stuff we really do not need. We can learn to ignore expensive enticements and concentrate on what really is important—a personal relationship with our Heavenly Father and doing His will.

♥ Read 1 Timothy 6:17-19. What advice does Paul give those who are rich?

_____

_____

Paul warns those who are rich not to be proud or to trust in their money. Instead, he tells them to trust in the living God. He tells rich people to use their money to do good works and to give generously to those in need. Great responsibility accompanies riches; therefore, those who have money are to be generous and provide many good deeds. The key to using money wisely is to use it for God's purposes and not accumulate it for ourselves (Luke 12:33). Does your money allow you to help others? If so, you are storing up treasures in heaven. But what if God asks you to sell everything? Would you do it?

♥ **Read Matthew 19:21-22. How do you respond to what Jesus tells the rich young man to do?**

_____

_____

♥ **Would you be willing to sell or liquidate everything you own to go serve God? Please explain.**

_____

In the Bible Jesus tells the rich young man to go and sell everything he has and give the money to the poor to have treasures in heaven. Does that mean all believers are to sell everything they own? What about the responsibility we have for the needs of our families? I believe our Heavenly Father will not ask every believer to sell everything, but if He asks you to do so, would you be willing to give up everything? I think it all boils down to our willingness to obey whatever God asks us to do. Our Heavenly Father will not allow anything between us and Him.

Our Heavenly Father did tell my husband and me to sell our home, give away most of our possessions, leave our precious children and grandchildren, and go overseas to love another group of people. Was this difficult? Yes and no. We miss our children and grandchildren terribly, but in our new culture He has given us other families to fill that void. Every place we have been, He has provided us with young people the ages of our children and grandchildren to play with and love on. Regarding the house and furnishings, actually that was the easy part, with the exception of my blue sofa. But the Father even provided me a very special family to whom I could give that. So through all of this I have learned not to hold too tightly to anything tangible, for it really belongs to Him. The relationships always are the most difficult for me to leave behind. Our immediate and extended family, our many precious friends—these are the people I miss and yearn to see and hug. But our Heavenly Father knows what is best for each of us.

I am amazed that most people think money is what brings happiness. Bless their hearts, will folks ever learn? Dear friends, don't crave riches; doing this will only leave you empty. Instead, listen to and follow the advice Paul gives us from First Timothy. Pursue it to refrain from the _love of money_.
- Realize you can't take it with you (6:7).
- Realize one day all riches will be gone (6:7, 17).
- Be content with what you have (6:8).
- Monitor what you are willing to do to get more money (6:9, 10).
- Love people more than money (6:11).
- Love God's work more than money (6:11).
- Freely share what you have with others (6:18).

A *faith that works* is a faith that trusts in our Heavenly Father and not in riches or money. Make sure the treasures you are storing up are worthy of heaven. Believe me, you will not regret it!

---♥--

All idolized treasure will soon perish.

Matthew Henry

Your Thoughts

Questions

Comments

Prayer Requests

Prayer Answers

Week 7, Day 5

Cheating Others

† **Heart Truths:**

Look, the wages you failed to pay the workmen who mowed your fields are crying out against you. The cries of the harvesters have reached the Lord Almighty (Jas. 5:4 NIV).

Today's Focus: James 5:4-6; Leviticus 19:13; Isaiah 5:8-9; Amos 8:4-5; Deuteronomy 24:14-15; Nehemiah 5:9-11; Jeremiah 22:13; Proverbs 3:27-28; 20:23; 1 Corinthians 12:26; Luke 16:19-31

Yesterday we studied about the worthlessness of storing up earthly treasures as opposed to accumulating heavenly treasures in the eternal Kingdom of God. Today we continue James' warnings to rich people. We will examine how wealth not only leads to greed and self-sufficiency, it also leads to exploiting other people and self-indulgency. So get your Bible and let's begin.

♥ **Read James 5:4-6. How do you respond to the warnings these verses give?**

_____

_____

James emphatically tells rich people to listen to the cries of the workers whom they have cheated out of their pay. The Lord has heard their cries against the rich people. The Lord Almighty has seen how the rich live in luxury and how they have condemned and even killed good people who have no power to defend themselves. The *good* people refer to the defenseless, poor laborers who cannot pay their debts and are thrown into prison. Thus, they are forced to sell all they have including selling their family members into slavery. Many of these poor people die of starvation; God calls this *murder*. Folks, we are warned that hoarding money does not escape God's notice; neither does exploiting people nor self-indulgency. Read further.

♥ **Read the following verses. Identify what is being said about employers paying wages to workers.**

Leviticus 19:13

_____

Deuteronomy 24:14-15

_____

163

Proverbs 3:27-28

Jeremiah 22:13

These verses explicitly tell employers to promptly pay their workers the wages due to them. If they do not, they take advantage of the workers and will be held accountable for the injustice they have caused them. Jeremiah identifies this behavior as *oppression*. Keep reading.

♥ Read Isaiah 5:8-9. Why do you think God, in these verses, condemns the wealthy?

Isaiah says the Lord Almighty has sealed the fate of the wealthy and that destruction is certain for them. Why? Because they have exploited other people by buying up property so others will have no place to live. Have no doubt; God will punish their sins. Look at the following example.

♥ Read Luke 16:19-31. What consequences does the rich man pay for his behavior?

♥ Do you have a person in your life that you know needs your help?

♥ If so, what have you done to help?

You are probably familiar with the story Jesus tells about the rich man and the beggar named Lazarus. From the Scripture we know Lazarus longs for scraps from the rich man's table, but the rich man ignores him. Consequently, when the rich man dies, he goes to eternal torment in hell. While there he begs for Lazarus to cool his tongue. Quite a change of events, wouldn't you say? The rich man does not go to hell because of his money. He goes to hell because he is selfish, self-indulgent, and refuses to help and care for Lazarus. Do you have a Lazarus in your life? What is your attitude about the blessings and/or money our Heavenly Father has allowed you to have? Are you selfish, or do you freely use what you have to help others?

♥ **Read Amos 8:4-5 and Proverbs 20:23. What do you think these verses say about cheating other people?**

_____

_____

Besides withholding a worker's pay, another way of taking advantage of people is by using dishonest scales. Merchants were said to actually look forward to cheating helpless people with false measures and weights on loaded, dishonest scales. Their only real interest is in themselves. The Lord despises double standards such as deceitful people using dishonest scales. But you say you never would be dishonest and cheat anyone? What about lying? Let's discuss this further.

♥ **Have you ever been dishonest in any of your transactions? Please explain.**

_____

_____

Dishonesty in itself is deceiving and works against us. When we are dishonest about something, we soon begin to believe the lie we have made up to be true. We even may lose the ability to tell the difference between the truth and the lie. The problem with believing our own lies is that we only deceive ourselves. In the process we alienate ourselves from God, because He despises all forms of dishonesty. We also lose credibility in our relationships. Now I know I am not the only one guilty of ever being dishonest in my lifetime. In fact, when I was growing up, I had a real problem with lying. To avoid severe physical discipline from my dad I quickly learned to lie. Actually, I would tell him what I thought he wanted to know, because he did not believe the truth when I tried to tell it. Not good! Why? I was deceiving only myself and making my Heavenly Father angry with me. Thankfully God has helped me to overcome this problem.

What about you? Have you ever been dishonest? Cheated on an exam? Cheated on your income tax? Exaggerated when telling something? Not reported everything? Told someone you were not at home when you were? Pretended to be asleep when you were not? Refused to answer the telephone or the door? The list could go on and on. Dear precious friends, dishonesty is cheating; lying can lead to oppression of other people. In other words cheating others is defrauding someone by deceitful means. Any dishonesty is severely warned against in God's Word. Dishonesty does not just apply to the wealthy; it applies to all of us who are believers. So what do we do if we are being dishonest?

♥ **Read Nehemiah 5:9-11. What does Nehemiah instruct the people to do?**

_____

_____

Our Heavenly Father always has been concerned with fairness, especially with the poor and oppressed. Imitate God's love in everything you do. Nehemiah says that the people are to walk in the fear of our God. They must restore their fields and homes and repay any interest they charged on their money, grain, wine, or olive oil. In other words caring for someone is much more important than is personal gain. Stay away from the lure of money and possessions. Live as Jesus lives, as He offers a life of obedience, service, and love. Folks, when another believer suffers, we all suffer (1 Cor. 12:26). Our responsibility is to help other believers and not to exploit them or be self-indulgent. A *faith that works* makes a practice of doing good deeds and helping the people around us who are in need. But how do we know when and how to help? We know by trusting our Heavenly Father to lead and show us all things. Is that what you are doing? If not, why not?

--- ♥ ---

And having thus chosen our course, let us renew our trust in God and go forward without fear.

Abraham Lincoln

Your Thoughts

Questions

Comments

Prayer Requests

Prayer Answers

Week 8
Victory 1: Faith Waits Patiently

Day 1
Wait Patiently for Jesus' Return

Day 2
Grumbling Again?

Day 3
Patience in Suffering

Day 4
Keep On Keeping On

Day 5
Say Yes *or* No; *That's Enough!*

Having completed our study on the *Seven Characteristics of Faith*, we will spend our final two weeks together studying about the *Two Victories of Faith*. This week we will delve into the *First Victory of Faith: Faith Waits Patiently for Jesus' Return*. In our final week we will probe into the *Second Victory of Faith: Faith Prays Faithfully* for ourselves and others. Wow! What an ending to our study that will be! As our lessons unfold this week, we will examine our own actions involving patience, waiting, grumbling, suffering, perseverance, swearing, and taking vows. Big topics, so hang in there as we go through these next few days. If you are to understand about having the faith to wait for Jesus' return, then examine these topics to see how they apply to your life. Do you have your Bible? Are you in your quiet place where you can pour out your heart to your Heavenly Father who hears and understands you more than anyone? Listen! He may speak in the hush of the early morning, in the silence of a whisper, or in the innermost part of your very soul. But know that in whichever way He chooses to speak to your heart and your mind, listen so you may hear Him.

Heart Truths
Day 1: James 5:8
Day 2: James 5:9
Day 3: James 5:10
Day 4: James 5:11
Day 5: James 5:12

Week 8, Day 1

Wait Patiently for Jesus' Return

Today's Focus: James 5:7-8; 2 Samuel 5:4-5; Genesis 29:20-30; 2 Thessalonians 1:4; 2:17; Romans 8:24-25; 12:12; Ephesians 6:13; Psalms 27:14; 37:7; 46:1; John 11:5-7; Isaiah 40:31; Acts 1:15-26; Proverbs 27:19; 24:12; 1 Thessalonians 5:2,14; 2 Peter 3:10; Matthew 24:45-47

As we begin this week's study, we observe James encouraging believers to patiently endure sufferings in view of the future coming of the Lord. The patience James describes is active and involves action; it is not passive. Believers are to persevere during suffering, love and care for each other, refuse to grumble about or criticize other people, and obey God by doing the work He calls us to do. As believers, we know our Heavenly Father has a special purpose for each of our lives. So what does waiting patiently for the Lord's return mean? How can that be accomplished? Look with me as we see what God's Word has to say.

♥ Read James 5:7-8. What does *wait patiently for the Lord's return* mean to you?

_____

_____

We have learned that *patience* means having the ability to bear trials without grumbling. OUCH! Do you complain or grumble as I have had a tendency to do at times? Grumbling is the subject of tomorrow's lesson, so I will leave that topic until then. We understand *patience* also means endurance and longsuffering. In fact it is a character trait of the fruit of the Spirit found in Galatians 5. *Waiting*, on the other hand, means to stay, to serve, or attend to. Actually *waiting* is an attitude of watchfulness. James shares with us the example of the farmer who eagerly looks for the rains in the fall and spring. The farmer patiently waits for the precious harvest to grow and ripen, because he can do nothing to hurry the growth process. However, for the farmer to ensure a good harvest, continuing to work his crops is necessary. James makes the analogy that we, too, can be patient and strengthen our hearts as we wait for the Lord's appearing. If our hearts are strengthened, then our capacity for endurance will be greater. Some translations use the term *stand firm* or *take courage* instead of *strengthening our hearts*. In reality you will recognize that the phrases can be used synonymously as we progress through this lesson. Can we do anything to make Jesus' return occur any faster? Of course not; we simply are to wait. But like the farmer we can do much work to bring God's Kingdom closer. Dig deeper with me.

♥ Read 2 Samuel 5:4-5. What do you think has to take place before David is ready to become king?

_____

_____

Sometimes persisting in patience is difficult. Look at the example of David; he does not begin to reign as king until he is 30-years old, even though Samuel anoints him as king when David is age 16. David has to *wait patiently* all those years for the fulfillment of God's promise. Our Heavenly Father always keeps His promises (Rom. 8:24-25). Even though the plan takes more time than we expect, God uses those waiting periods to strengthen our characters and to better prepare us for the service He calls us to do.

♥ Read the following verses and answer this question: What are you capable of achieving in your life because you are willing to wait patiently?

Genesis 29:20-30

_____

2 Thessalonians 1:4

_____

Patience is extremely difficult at times; however, it is the <u>key</u> to achieving our goals. In Genesis we see that Jacob works seven years for Rachel to become his wife. Then he is tricked into marrying Leah. Consequently he ends up with two wives within two weeks of each other but only after he agrees to work an additional seven years for his father-in-law, Laban. Fair? Maybe not! God's plan? Perhaps! I cannot make that judgment. I only can observe God using those marriages for His glory and purpose to create the 12 tribes of Israel.

In Second Thessalonians we recognize that patience is the <u>key</u> to surviving trials and persecution. Jacob faithfully endures to receive Rachel as his wife. Evidently he believes she is someone worthy of working and waiting for. As believers we know from experiences that God uses our trials for our own good and for His glory. Since our Heavenly Father is patient with us, we also can be patient with others (1 Thess. 5:14) and be patient in times of troubles (Rom. 12:12). Please read further.

♥ **Read Psalms 27:14 and 37:7. How do you respond to the instructions these verses give?**

_____

_____

David certainly can speak from experience when he tells us to wait patiently for the Lord to act. David waits on God to fulfill His promise for him to reign as king. Waiting on our Heavenly Father to act is not easy. Sometimes we think He is not answering our prayers or He doesn't understand the urgency of our problems. But I have experienced many times in my life in which His timing always is perfect (John 11:5-7) and is definitely worth the wait. Here is one of those experiences.

When my husband and I left the States to serve overseas, our house had not sold. People in our new location did not believe we would go overseas if our house had not sold, but we did. After several months passed, our Heavenly Father sold it. We all rejoiced. Yes, we had to wait patiently, but we observed God using our belief to trust Him and go where He was leading us as a testimony to others of His glory, provisions, and promises. He expects us all to wait patiently. This not only will make us stronger, it will strengthen and have a positive influence on others.

♥ **Read Isaiah 40:31. What will happen to you if you are willing to wait patiently on the Lord?**

_____

_____

How I love this verse! Those of us who wait on the Lord will find new strength. We will fly high on wings like eagles. We will run and not grow weary; we will walk and not faint. Hallelujah! God will keep His promises if we wait on Him. He will rise us up above all of our circumstances. Frequently we spend those times of waiting being taught or renewed or being refreshed. Usually our blessings are a direct result of having to go through a trial period of waiting. It may not be fun, but it makes us grow.

♥ **Read Acts 1:15-26. What are you to do while you wait on the Lord?**

_____

_____

In these verses we observe that the church is having a business meeting to appoint a new disciple. While it waits, the members pray, seek God's guidance, and get organized. That is also what we can do. When you wait, don't sit around and twiddle your thumbs. Instead pray and ask your Heavenly Father for His guidance. Don't run ahead of Him! He will instruct you if you are patient and wait. Believe me, the waiting is worth everything!

♥ Read Proverbs 27:19. How do you respond to what this verse says about your heart?

_____

_____

According to Proverbs the heart reflects the person. We have heard remarks such as: a good heart, cruel heart, pure heart, hard heart, soft heart, compassionate heart, kind heart, and so on. What kind of heart do you believe you have? Scripture says God knows all hearts and sees yours (Prov. 24:12). Paul prays for our Lord Jesus and God our Father to comfort our hearts and give us strength in every good thing we do and say (2 Thess. 2:17). Paul realizes we cannot do it on our own. To withstand the attacks of Satan, depend on God to strengthen your heart (Eph. 6:13). God is our refuge and strength and is always ready to help us and provide strength in every circumstance (Ps. 46:1). We understand that things don't happen in our strength but in His strength.

♥ Read 1 Thessalonians 5:2 and 2 Peter 3:10. According to these verses when will the day of the Lord arrive?

_____

Always be aware that no one knows when Jesus will return. According to these verses His arrival will be unexpected like a thief in the night; we all will be surprised. For unbelievers it will be a terrible time, but for believers we will rejoice because we have waited patiently for His return. Be ready at all times. How are you to be ready? What are you to do? How do you wait for Jesus' return?

♥ Read Matthew 24:45-47. What does Jesus tell you to do while you wait for His return?

_____

_____

While we wait for Jesus to return, we are to obey God's Word, care for and help other people, and do the work He has planned for us here on earth. We are not to waste time; instead, we are to resist sin and live in such a way we will please Him when He arrives. Keep the goal of His return in your minds as we pray for strength and endurance to survive trials and persecution. To have a _faith that works_, endure and have your heart strengthened through the Lord Jesus as you wait patiently for His return. Can you say with me, "Come, Lord Jesus"?

--- ♥ ---

Hallelujah! My dear sibling in Christ, as surely as Jesus died and rose again, He will return.

Beth Moore

Your Thoughts

Questions

Comments

Prayer Requests

Prayer Answers

Week 8, Day 2

Grumbling Again

Today's Focus: James 5:9; John 6:43; 1 Corinthians 4:1-5; 10:10; Luke 15:1-2; Philippians 2:14; 4:5; 1 Peter 4:7; 1 John 4:4; Numbers 14:2, 36-37; 16:41-49; Acts 6:1; Revelation 3:20; Matthew 7:1-5; 12:36; 25:31-46

Have you ever grumbled when things go wrong? Have you ever blamed someone other than yourself for your problems? Have you ever complained about someone or something without hearing both sides of the story? Have you ever ridiculed another person because he or she was offensive to you? What little things about others just irritate you to death? Does this happen when you are driving and someone darts in front of your car? How about when someone is rude to you or when you perceive some trait in another person that mirrors yourself? What do you do about it? Does your reaction reflect the Lord Jesus? Do your words reflect what Jesus would say? Tough questions, right? I know they are for me. Let's examine what James says about grumbling.

♥ Read James 5:9. Why do you think James says we are not to grumble?

_____

_____

♥ Have you ever had a problem with grumbling? If so, explain.

_____

_____

James emphatically tells us not to grumble about each other. He further states that if we do, the Lord Jesus will judge us. James reminds us that Jesus is standing at the door! When things do not go to suit us, we tend to grumble against and even blame others for our problems. Why? Is this our old sin nature emerging? I guess we become defensive and do not want to own our part of the responsibility. However, our grumbling and blame cause some real problems. Let's see why.

♥ Read Numbers 14:2, 36-37; 16:41-49. How did you respond to these verses about the causes of grumbling and complaining?

_____

_____

In these verses we see Korah and his followers citing an open rebellion against Moses by their grumbling and complaining. Even after the earth swallows them up for their behavior and attitude, the Israelites start grumbling all over again. The negative attitude of a person leads to more and more rebellion and gets him or her into greater trouble. Grumbling is a vicious cycle! Rebellion begins with dissatisfaction, then grumbling, followed by bitterness, which leads to more open rebellion and hostility. Beware! This cycle leads to separation from God and final destruction. That's why many verses in God's Word say grumbling or complaining is forbidden (John 6:43; 1 Cor. 10:10; Phil. 2:14). See Illustration 2, The Vicious Cycle of Grumbling, on page 222 in the Appendix.

Grumbling is one of the sins of which my Heavenly Father convicted me many years ago. When I was growing up, I had a very negative mother. Bless her heart, everything she said was based on a complaint or a negative comment. She even bragged about achieving the title of "Class Grumbler" when she graduated from high school. How sad that she took pride in something so negative as grumbling! Consequently for my entire lifetime I have struggled to produce positive thoughts and words rather than negative ones. This has not been easy, as the old tendencies remain. Satan is everpresent to remind me to complain or grumble. So through Scripture such as, . . . *Greater is He that is in you than He that is in the world* (1 John 4:4 NAS) and through lots of prayer, the daily struggle is defeated! This is a choice I make every day of my life! I pray it is not so for you.

♥ Read Acts 6:1 and Luke 15:1-2. In these verses what is the topic of these peoples' complaints?

_____

_____

Often we think of the early church as being perfect. I chuckle, because if I were a member of the early church, it certainly would not be perfect. What about you? We see the early church having the same problems with grumbling and complaining as we have today. In Acts we see rumblings of discontent in the distribution of food to the widows. In Luke the Pharisees and teachers complain about Jesus associating with despicable people. Even Adam blames Eve for his sin; she in turn blames the serpent. We tend to excuse our sins by blaming others. We even complain about someone's faithfulness by jumping to conclusions and calling ourselves "fruit inspectors". Look at the next verse.

♥ Read 1 Corinthians 4:1-5. What is the warning you are to heed?

_____

_____

Only God knows a person's heart; He is the only one qualified to judge a person's faithfulness. Paul tells us to be careful not to jump to conclusions as to whether or not someone is faithful. Who do we think we are anyway? What arrogance we have at times! When the Lord returns, He will bring our deepest secrets to light and will reveal our private motives. I don't know about you, but I sure don't want my words and my attitude hung out on the line for all to see. Read on.

♥ **Read Matthew 7:1-5; 12:36; 25:31-46. From these verses what warnings does Jesus give you about your actions toward others?**

_____

_____

In earlier lessons we talked about judging others and the consequences that follow. However, the same thing applies here as well. When Jesus tells us to stop judging, He is warning us about our own negative motives and conduct. As believers we are called to be discerning, not negative, and to realize God—not us—is the final judge. Remember that on judgment day you will give account of every idle word and perhaps every complaining word, so be careful of the words you speak. Allow the Holy Spirit to fill you with new motives and a positive attitude. The real evidence of your belief is in your actions and how you treat other people. So how do you treat other people?

♥ **Read Philippians 4:5 and 1 Peter 4:7. As you wait for Jesus' return, what is your attitude and behavior to reflect?**

_____

_____

Because the Lord will return soon, be considerate in all you do and say. Jesus is near to us; He is standing at our doors knocking. He says if we open the doors of our hearts, He will enter and share a meal with each of us (Rev. 3:20). Jesus wants to fellowship with us; this gives us ultimate joy because He will dwell with us. However, we may not totally comprehend this ultimate joy until Jesus' second coming. Until then, be fair-minded and love others—believers and unbelievers. Peter further tells us we are to be serious and disciplined in our prayers. Praying regularly to maintain our relationship with our Heavenly Father is highly important. Through His leadership we respond to the needs of others. Invest your time and talents where they will make a difference eternally. Therefore, to have a _faith that works_ till Jesus returns, be people of prayer who are willing to stop grumbling and complaining. I surely am; I hope you are, too.

-- ♥ --

For the sake of fellowship, you must destroy your arsenal of relational nuclear weapons, including condemning, belittling, comparing, labeling, insulting, condescending, and being sarcastic.

Rick Warren

Your Thoughts

Questions

Comments

Prayer Requests

Prayer Answers

Week 8, Day 3

Patience in Suffering

Today's Focus: James 5:10-11; 2 Thessalonians 1:4; John 9:1; 1 Peter 3:17; 5:10; 2:7; Acts 13:8-11; 14:19; 16:19-24; 1 John 2:15-17; Romans 7:18-24; 8:28; 1 Corinthians 2:3; 2 Corinthians 1:8; Hebrews 12:5-6; 2 Samuel 4:4; Jeremiah 37:11-16; Job 1:21; 2:7; John 9:1-3.

In our study this week we defined *patience* to mean endurance and longsuffering as well as having the ability to bear trials without grumbling. We also discovered that *patience* is the key to surviving trials, persecution, and suffering (2 Thess. 1:4). In our study today we will elaborate on the concept of patience in suffering. As we explore some biblical examples of suffering, we will identify the different kinds of suffering, the purposes of suffering, and the responses we can have to suffering. Throughout Scripture we have observed many godly people suffering persecution. These include Joseph, Moses, David, Jeremiah, Job, Peter, and Paul. Because of limited time we will keep our examples to only two of these great men. Let's begin by reading James.

♥ **Read James 5:10-11. What does being patient in the face of suffering mean?**

_____

_____

None of us likes to suffer. In fact we tend to try to avoid suffering at all costs. James doesn't say God will remove our suffering, but he does encourage us by referring to the suffering of the prophets. As we examine these men of God, we realize our Heavenly Father does not necessarily remove suffering, but He goes with us through all suffering. James indicates we are not alone and that we will be blessed if we persevere! Read further.

♥ **Read 1 Peter 3:17. After you read this verse, respond by naming some of the ways you or someone close to you has suffered.**

_____

_____

Peter tells us that suffering for doing good is better than is suffering for doing wrong! Actually three main kinds of suffering exist: physical, mental, and spiritual.

• **Physical suffering** involves a part of our body that may either break down or become injured. It could result from the development of an internal problem such as a terminal illness; from an external problem such as an automobile accident (2 Sam. 4:4); from a congenital deformity such as a cleft lip (John 9:1); or from Satan as he is allowed to inflict our bodies (Job 2:7). Any suffering has the ability to bring much pain to believers.

• **Mental suffering** can be caused by fear, despair, grief, bitterness, torment, worry, discouragement, oppression, or anything else we allow to affect our minds or our hearts (1 Cor. 2:3; 2 Cor. 1:8). Warranted or unwarranted, mental suffering can be much more intense than physical suffering can be.

• **Spiritual suffering** comes from the temptations of the world (1 John 2:15-17), our old sinful natures (Rom. 7:18-24), or the influences of Satan (Acts 13:8-11). Spiritual suffering either will draw you closer to God or drive you further away. Actually it is your choice! Have you experienced suffering in your life?

♥ **Read Job 2:7. What does Satan do when he leaves God's presence?**

_____

_____

Rather than ask ourselves why God permits this to happen, maybe we need to try to see suffering from our Heavenly Father's viewpoint. Believe it or not, understand that suffering has a purpose is important. Before you read any further, I think trying to answer this question is crucial.

♥ **What purpose could God have in allowing His children to suffer?**

_____

_____

If you are a parent, what purpose could you possibly have for taking the telephone or car away from your teen-ager? What purpose could you have for allowing a younger child to go to his or her room or into "time-out" for bad behavior? If you are single, what purpose could you have for not getting involved with the spouse of another person? Would you agree that you have very good reasons for your behavior? Well, so does our Heavenly Father when suffering is concerned. Let's look at several verses for some possible reasons God allows believers to suffer.

God allows His children to suffer to—
• receive His promises (Heb. 10:36);
• silence the devil (Job 1:9-11);
• glorify God (John 9:1-3);

- make us more like Jesus (Phil. 3:10);
- teach us dependence (John 15:1-5);
- refine our lives (Ps. 66:10-12);
- rebuke our sin (Heb. 12:5-9);
- enlarge our ministry toward others (2 Cor. 1:3-7).

Just a loving earthly father or mother punishes a misbehaving child, so does our Heavenly Father. Suffering actually can develop patience, joy, knowledge, and make us more mature in our walk with God. We read that God allows Satan to torment Job to demonstrate Job's love for God because of Who He is, rather than for what he can get materially from Him. All suffering produces some form of stress in our lives. Learning how to deal with it is important. Let's read further and see how we are to respond to suffering.

♥ **Read Job 1:21. As a believer what do you think the Bible says about your response to suffering?**

_____

_____

Job is a man of integrity! When he loses everything, what does he do? He falls to the ground and worships God. Wow! What an example for us to follow! How would you respond if you had lost everything? As you know, we have a choice in how we respond to situations. We can hate them and brush them off too lightly, or we can weaken under them and treat them too seriously (Heb. 12:5-6). However, the better response is to be patient and learn from situations and respond in the same manner that Job does. Actually this latter response is probably the reaction God desires for us to have. Suffering is a two-sided coin. On one side we can view suffering as being from God to bring out the best in us. On the other side suffering can be viewed as being from Satan to bring out the worst in us. Whichever way we choose to view it, remember we must commit our suffering to God, be patient in it, and realize He is faithful to work things out for our good (Rom. 8:28).

♥ **Read the following verses; identify how Jeremiah and Paul suffer. How can you relate to the sufferings they experience?**

Jeremiah 37:11-16

_____

_____

Acts 14:19 and 16:19-24

_____

_____

In God's Word we find many examples of believers who suffer for the sake of righteousness. Among them are Jeremiah and Paul. Jeremiah is persecuted by his own family; plotted against by his own hometown; rejected and ridiculed by his peers; and arrested, beaten, and accused of treason. In naming only a few of the sufferings Paul experiences we observe that he is plotted against, stoned and left for dead, beaten and jailed, ridiculed, falsely accused, bitten by a serpent, and forsaken by all. These men are obedient and faithful despite the hardships they endure.

In looking at these two men and how they deal with their suffering, I become ashamed at the manner in which I have responded to some of my past sufferings. As a believer, commit your pain and suffering to your Holy Father, Who loves you and is faithful to walk with you through all of your storms. James tells you to count it all joy when you experience trials and sufferings. So when you are tempted to think that patience in suffering is impossible, remember: you have a God Who is in charge of making the impossible become possible.

♥ **Read 1 Peter 5:10. What are you promised after you have suffered for a little while?**

_____

_____

As mentioned in an earlier lesson, this is such an awesome verse! But let's review it again. Our Heavenly Father promises us after we have suffered for a little while, He will perfect, confirm, strengthen, and establish us. WOW! As you know, *to perfect us* means we will have an extreme degree of excellence. *To confirm us* means we will be made steadfast and sure. *To strengthen us* means we will have resistant power. *To establish us* means we have a permanent condition. Imagine that—we as believers will be perfected, confirmed, strengthened, and established. Hang in there, my friend; the best is yet to be! To have a *faith that works*, be faithful to obey God; be patient in your sufferings. You really do have a light at the end of the tunnel. Can you see it yet?

-- ♥ --

If you are going to be used by God, He will take you through a multitude of experiences that are not meant for you at all, they are meant to make you useful in His hands, and to enable you to understand what transpires in other souls so that you will never be surprised at what you come across.

Oswald Chambers

Jesus said, "God blesses you when you are mocked and persecuted and lied about because you are my followers. Be happy about it! Be very glad! For a great reward awaits you in heaven. And remember, the ancient prophets were persecuted, too"

(Mt. 5:11-12).

Your Thoughts

Questions

Comments

Prayer Requests

Prayer Answers

Week 8, Day 4

Keep On Keeping On

† Heart Truths:

As you know, we consider blessed those who have persevered . . . The Lord is full of compassion and mercy
(Jas. 5:11 NIV).

Today's Focus: James 1:2-4,12; 5:11; Genesis 32:26; Nehemiah 4:6; Job 19:25-27; 42:10-17; Matthew 10:22; Mark 13:13; Luke 11:8-10; 1 Corinthians 9:24-27; Romans 2:7; Revelation 3:10; Philippians 3:12-14; 1 Timothy 6:11; 2 Timothy 4:6-8

Many of you are survivors. Like I am, you are very familiar with the concept of "keep on keeping on"—of never giving up. Perhaps most of you have seen the cartoon picture of the bird trying to pull the worm out of the dirt and the worm holding on for his life. Even though this cartoon is humorous, it is a dramatic picture of perseverance! Did you know that our Heavenly Father actually commands us to persevere (Rev. 3:10)? In our study today James switches from patience to perseverance. His words move around full-circle as he tells us that our troubles can teach us perseverance (Jas. 1:2-4,12). But what is *perseverance*?

According to the *Life Application Dictionary/Concordance*, *perseverance* means to endure hardships with patience. Looks as though a relationship exists between patience and perseverance. How interesting! Could perseverance be an expansion of patience? I think so, but determination and persistence can also describe perseverance. The persistence for believers to continue in the face of obstacles is a positive trait. Let's look at God's Word.

♥ **From the following verses answer these two questions: (1) What biblical truths can you identify? (2) Why are you commanded to persevere?**

Genesis 32:26

_____

_____

Nehemiah 4:6

_____

_____

Matthew 10:22

_____

_____

182

In Genesis, Jacob wrestles with God and refuses to let Him go until God agrees to bless him. We observe God being pleased with Jacob's persistence and as a result changes his name to *Israel,* which means one who struggles with God. The biblical truth in this passage is that perseverance makes our character stronger.

♥ Do you think perseverance will make your character stronger? Why or why not?

_____

_____

In Nehemiah we read that the people are persistent and work diligently to complete the building of the wall. They do not give up but persevere even in the face of opposition. Thus we see that perseverance can be a weapon against opposition and even discouragement. What do you think of this truth? Could perseverance be a weapon for you against opposition and discouragement? I hope so!

In Matthew, Jesus says if we endure to the end, we will be saved. Dear friends, please realize that enduring to the end is not a way to be saved; instead, it is evidence of our salvation and commitment to our Lord Jesus. Are you willing to make the commitment to endure and persevere to the end? Perseverance is a result of a dedicated life. Let your emphasis be on obeying God and being persistent. But how do we know in which areas to persevere? Let's look further.

♥ Read Mark 13:13. In what area does Jesus tell you to persevere?

_____

_____

Jesus says everyone will hate us because of our allegiance to Him, but He also tells us to endure to the end. As you know, trials separate true believers from fair-weather believers. Therefore, persevere in your faith, because you know that the guarantee of your salvation keeps you strong during trials.

♥ Read Luke 11:8-10. In what area does this suggest that you persevere?

_____

_____

Jesus teaches His disciples about being persistent in their prayers. He says persevering in prayer does many things: Prayer changes our hearts and minds, helps us understand and communicate the greatness of our need, helps us overcome our insensitivity, and helps us recognize the work of our Heavenly Father in answering our prayers.

♥ **Read Romans 2:7. In what area does this suggest that you persevere?**

_____

_____

Paul says we will receive eternal life if we persevere in doing what is good. When you commit your life fully to your Heavenly Father, you desire to do His will. Therefore, good deeds become byproducts of what He has done for you. Paul instructs Timothy to pursue a godly life, along with faith, love, perseverance, and gentleness (1 Tim. 6:11). Therefore, like Timothy, also persevere in these areas and especially in your faith, in your prayer life, and in doing good deeds.

♥ **Read 1 Corinthians 9:24-27. From these verses how do you respond to the promise we have if we persevere?**

_____

_____

Paul uses the illustration of winning a race if we persist with the end in mind because our prize will be eternal. Our Heavenly Father calls us to our heavenly home if we persevere (Phil. 3:12-14). Paul's goal is to forget the past and to look forward to what lies ahead. In this passage he wants to reach the end of the race and receive the prize of God calling him to his heavenly home. Paul concludes that he has fought a good fight, finished the race, and is looking forward to the prize — the crown of righteousness (2 Tim. 4:6-8). What about you, my friend? Do you want to leave your past behind you, persevere toward your heavenly reward, and receive your crown of righteousness? I surely do. One of the greatest desires of my heart is to hear my Heavenly Father some day say, "_Well done, my good and faithful servant._" I pray it will be so.

♥ **Read James 5:11 and Job 19:25-27; 42:10-17. What promise do you have if you continue to persevere?**

_____

_____

Most of you are familiar with the story of Job and how he maintains his integrity despite of all the persecution and bodily harm. According to James, Job is an example of a man who endures patiently. God blesses Job in the end after he has prayed for his friends. In fact God gives Job twice as much as he had before because of His tenderness and mercy. Don't ever give up, my dear friend. When you persevere, our Heavenly Father will bless you — that is His promise. A _faith that works_ is a belief that "keeps on keeping on" — in faith, in prayer, and in doing good deeds!

---------------------------------------♥---------------------------------------

When we are caught in trauma's grip, whatever shape or size it may be, we need the kind of fortitude to endure that is born of ultimate hope: the patience of the good farmer, a determined faith that perseveres in the belief that one day the trials will be over.

Jill Briscoe

Your Thoughts

Questions

Comments

Prayer Requests

Prayer Answers

Week 8, Day 5

Say Yes or No; That's Enough!

Today's Focus: James 5:12; Exodus 20:7; Leviticus 5:4; Proverbs 20:25; Numbers 30:1-2; Judges 11:30-40; Matthew 5:33-37; Mark 6:22-28

My spirit hurts when I observe how people, even believers, flippantly use the name of our Lord Jesus and our Heavenly Father. Enjoying a television program or watching a movie or video has become rare without hearing some form of filthy, bad language. What have we allowed the world to do to us? Why do we tolerate such horrible language? We have become so desensitized to it. How do I know? Well, I can inquire from friends about the content of a new movie and will be told the movie is good and as far as they remember it has no bad language. Unfortunately, when I go see it, rent it, or buy it, Lord forgive us, the horrible words are there. Then we have the problem with our making empty vows and/or promises. We say things too quickly without regard to the consequences our words may bring. But these problems are not new; they were happening back in James' day. That is why he addresses them. Let's see what God's Word says.

♥ **Read James 5:12. In this verse what do you think James is saying to you?**

_____

_____

♥ **Have you ever had a time in your life in which you or someone close to you had a problem with swearing or making empty vows or promises?** _____
How did you deal with the experience?

_____

_____

James is very blunt with his remarks. He tells you never to take an oath or swear by heaven or earth or anything else, because doing this is a sin. You will be condemned. Instead simply say "*yes* or *no*"! Are you a person of your word? Do you exaggerate or lie? If you avoid telling lies, then do you tell half-truths or omit the truth? Are you a person others can trust and believe that your word is true? Do people believe what you say? If not, why not? Believers are supposed to be honest where a simple "*yes* or *no*" from our mouths is sufficient. Read further.

♥ Read Exodus 20:7. What does this third commandment tell you?

_____

_____

As you know, the Ten Commandments are designed to lead the nation of Israel to a life of holiness. In the third commandment our Heavenly Father tells us that His name is very special because it is His personal identity, just like your name is your personal identity. For someone to misuse His name as a curse or to swear by it with a vow places that person in danger of eternal punishment. Remember, my friend, this is a commandment; to break it means punishment. The manner in which we use God's name communicates how we really feel about Him. Do we respect His name and use it appropriately, or do we use it lightly? Do we praise or worship His name, or do we curse or jest with it? How do you feel if someone curses you? I know what this does to me; it hurts my spirit!

Several years ago when my children were young, we went to visit a new friend. Before our visit we were not aware that she had freshly painted her home. As we entered the foyer, one of my children accidentally touched a freshly painted wall. I was so surprised when the new friend immediately cursed me with some really hurtful words. As quickly as I could, I grabbed my children and left her home. Yes, I forgave her and asked God to do the same. But think about it—if that incident hurt me so much, how much more does swearing and using our Father's name disrespectfully hurt the Lord our God?

♥ Read Matthew 5:33-37. Why do you think Jesus is teaching about vows?

_____

_____

Jesus tells you <u>not</u> to make any vows, but if you do, not to break them. Instead, carry out any vow you have made to the Lord. Jesus reminds us that nothing we swear by is acceptable. Heaven is God's throne, the earth is His footstool, and Jerusalem is the city of the great King. So we can swear by nothing that does not directly affect our Holy God. As you know, vows are common in Jesus' day; keeping them is very important. Why? To keep a vow builds trust in relationships with other people. However, the Bible condemns making vows casually. Jesus also tells us that a simple *yes* or *no* is enough! If you are known as a faithful, trustworthy person, then your word is enough. Have you sworn to do something and realized how foolish your words were? Did you follow through with what you swore to do? Let's see what happens when we make rash vows.

♥ **Read Leviticus 5:4. How do you respond to the dangers of making rash vows?**

_____

_____

God's Word tells us if we make a rash vow of any kind, whether for good or bad, we will be considered guilty even if we were not fully aware of what we were doing at the time. God takes vows very seriously and requires us to carry them out. Making a rash promise to God before counting the cost is dangerous (Prov. 20:25). Quite often our intentions may be good, but because vows or promises are so difficult to keep, we are better off not making them at all because of the potential consequences. In the following two examples look at what happens:

♥ **Read Judges 11:30-40. What are the consequences of Jephthah's vow?**

_____

_____

♥ **Read Mark 6:22-28. What are the consequences of Herod Antipas' vow?**

_____

_____

Jephthah's vow brings him unspeakable grief. Whether he actually murders his daughter or never allows her to marry is up for theological debate. However, without thinking he makes a vow. That vow may result in his sacrificing his very own daughter. Sometimes when we make them, our vows even may sound spiritual; instead, they produce only guilt and frustration when we are forced to fulfill them. Our Heavenly Father wants our obedience today and not an empty promise for the future.

Herod Antipas' vow to give the daughter of Herodias anything she requests results in his ordering the death of John the Baptist. Vows are very powerful and can lead to sin. Be careful to avoid making vows. If you make a vow, be sure to weigh the consequences of keeping or breaking it.

♥ **Read Numbers 30:1-2. What do these verses remind you?**

_____

_____

Moses reminds the people that if a vow is made to the Lord or a pledge under oath, then they must never break it and must do exactly what they say they will do. In olden times a person's word was a binding contract. Breaking it meant mistrust and broken relationships. What about today? Are broken promises harmful today? Of course they are. Strengthening our words with an oath is not necessary. Our word should be all that is required. *"Simply let your 'Yes' be 'Yes,' and your 'No' be 'No;' anything beyond this comes from the evil one"* (Mt. 5:37 NIV).

What about taking an oath in court? I don't believe James is prohibiting us from taking an oath in court. After all perjury is a serious offense. Instead I believe James is referring to swearing and making careless oaths and promises without thinking through the consequences. It involves using words that make a mockery out of the truth and are disrespectful to our Heavenly Father's name. For believers to take a stand against profanity, swearing, and the flippant use of God's name is imperative. Remember, to have a *faith that works*, we can stand on the truth of our words and refuse to swear or take an oath. What about you? Are you standing up for what's right?

---♥ --

The Lord will not hold him guiltless that takes His name in vain.
Matthew Henry

Your Thoughts

Questions

Comments

Prayer Requests

Prayer Answers

Week 9
Victory 2: Faith Prays Faithfully

Day 1
Prayers in Suffering

Day 2
Prayers for the Sick

Day 3
Prayers of Confession

Day 4
Power of Prayer

Day 5
Confronting Believers

This is it—our final week together. I did not realize I would have such mixed emotions, both of sadness and happiness—sadness because our time together will soon be over; happiness because I have learned much and pray you have, too. This week will conclude our study of James as we concentrate on the *Second Victory of Faith: Faith Prays Faithfully.* As I have said, prayer is one of my very favorite subjects! Praying faithfully is very important, because that is the lifeline to our relationship with our Heavenly Father. Prayer is powerful; that power is available to us when we regularly enter into His presence. Our Heavenly Father wants us to talk with Him; in fact, He even commands that we do. This is not an option! God wants us to always pray <u>first</u> about everything and never make prayer our last resort. This week, we will discuss how to pray effectively and powerfully for ourselves and for others. Our last day will have a slightly different focus on prayer, as it relates to confronting a straying believer—not easy, but necessary! Prayer—what an awesome ending to our time together! Speaking of prayer, are you in your secret closet in which you can pour out your heart and be yourself? I hope so, as that is where your Heavenly Father will meet you. Pray, listen! He is speaking to you.

Heart Truths
Day 1: James 5:13
Day 2: James 5:14-15a
Day 3: James 5:16
Day 4: James 5:17
Day 5: James 5:19-20

Week 9, Day 1

Prayers in Suffering

Today's Focus: James 1:5; 4:2-3; 5:13; Matthew 6:5-13; 7:7-8; 1 Thessalonians 5:18; Psalms 9:1; 18:3; 100; 147:7; 150:1; Philippians 4:6-7; Colossians 3:16

Once again James travels full circle in his book. In chapter one James issues a call to prayer when he urges us to ask for wisdom. In chapter four James gives us two warnings: to have the right motives when we pray and never to use prayer for selfish purposes. This week in chapter five James instructs us in how to have an effective prayer life. He mentions that all the main components of prayer include praise, thanksgiving, petition, confession, and commitment. Then James connects these components with suffering, healing, forgiveness, power, and confrontation. How awesome! In today's study we will focus on prayers in suffering. You will recall that last week we discussed the importance of having patience in suffering. However, understand that prayer is the main key that unlocks faith, which enables us to have the patience we need to go through any type of suffering. So let's begin by examining how prayer affects us personally.

♥ **Read James 5:13. How did you respond to what James says you are to do if you are suffering?**

_____

_____

James says if we suffer, we are to pray, be cheerful, and sing praises. Now wait just a minute! Does he mean if I am in severe pain, I am to be cheerful and sing praises? What do you think? How did you respond to the above question? We always have something for which to be thankful. Maybe it is not the severe pain at the time, but look around and ask yourself what you see God doing to get you through your current experience. What has He reminded you of lately? Please notice that this verse doesn't say to have others pray for us; instead it tells us to pray for ourselves. Let's see what that means.

The Greek word for *prayer* is *euche,* pronounced *yoo khay.* It means a wish expressed as a petition to God. To me prayer means much more than making a wish or a request. It is not all about asking, even though that may be part of it. Let me explain. Prayer is a worship experience because of having a relationship with my Heavenly Father. It is sharing my life, my deepest desires, my faults, my concerns, my relationships, and my innermost self with my Heavenly Father. Prayer means communicating with my Creator Who loves me so much He gave up His only Son that I may be forgiven. It is having the only real Father I have ever known. When I pray to my Heavenly Father, I sense His presence and know beyond a shadow of a doubt He hears me in spite of all my failures and weaknesses. Prayer is almost impossible to put into words. All I know is, when I get frustrated or self-absorbed or worried, I can fall on my knees, enter into His throne room, and bow prostrate at His feet. I can imagine myself curling up in His lap with His powerful arms around me and sensing the very warmth of His presence. This gives me such an indescribable peace I hardly have the words to express it. All I know in my simplicity is that when I am in my Father's presence, He is there with me and I am His child. Sometimes when I think of this, the tears cannot be controlled. It is awesome, it is healing, it is cleansing, it is comforting, and it is an unexplainable sense of His presence. What is prayer to you? Let's see what Jesus says about prayer.

♥ **Read Matthew 6:5-13. From these verses what does Jesus teach you to do when you pray?**

_____

_____

When Jesus teaches about prayer, He emphasizes private communication with God. He tells us to go alone into our rooms and close the doors and pray to our Heavenly Father in secret. Jesus further instructs us to refrain from babbling on and on but instead to use the "model prayer" as our guide. Jesus says to praise and adore our Heavenly Father, to confess our sins and ask for His forgiveness, to pray for His will and work to be accomplished, to ask Him to provide for our daily needs, to help us with our daily struggles, to deliver us from Satan, and to thank Him for His care and blessings. Jesus also says that God requires us to persist as we pray and never to give up our efforts to seek Him. Actually we are commanded to pray with the promise that if we ask, we will receive; if we seek, we will find; and if we knock, He will open the door (Mt. 7:7-8). Wow! What a promise! However, along with praying when we suffer, James mentions we also are to sing praises. Aren't praise and thanksgiving two of the main components of prayer? Why do we need to praise God in prayer when we are suffering? Let's read further.

♥ **Read Psalms 9:1 and Psalms 150:1. According to these verses exactly what are you doing when you praise God?**

_____

_____

According to David we are to praise the Lord with all of our hearts. To praise our Heavenly Father is to acknowledge His glory and excellence. It differs from thanksgiving, which describes what God has done for us rather than Who He really is. Only God is worthy of our praise (Ps. 18:3). Praise is telling our Heavenly Father how much we appreciate His holiness, grace, mercy, goodness, and kindness. It is an act of worshiping Him in spirit, truth, and love. It is the realization of who He really is. It is giving Him glory in all things. It is praising Him from a grateful heart in spite of our circumstances.

♥ **Read Colossians 3:16 and Psalms 147:7. In what ways do you praise God?**

_____

_____

We can praise our Heavenly Father with our spoken words. We can sing praises to Him as we pray and worship. We can sing with or without musical instruments, as true praise springs from a grateful heart. We can get on our knees or stand up or lift up our arms or close our eyes or all of the above. The posture is not what's important; it is the attitude of our hearts; it is whatever way draws you into His presence. For me, I have a deep need to meet with my Father in the early morning hours on my knees; then I know He is with me throughout the day. What about you? In what way do you enjoy praising your Heavenly Father?

♥ **Read 1 Thessalonians 5:18. What does this verse command you to do?**

_____

_____

♥ **Have you had a time in your life in which you expressed true thankfulness to God in a situation that was happening to you or a close family member? What were the results?**

_____

_____

That's right—being thankful is not an option either. We are commanded to always be thankful no matter what happens, for this is God's will for us who are in Christ Jesus. We have already studied in a previous lesson that Paul is not teaching us to thank God <u>for</u> everything but instead to thank God <u>in</u> everything. Big difference! We know when evil surfaces, we can be thankful for the presence of our Heavenly Father, who will walk with us through whatever suffering we may have. I've tested the waters and know He walks with me through those waters, especially when I am thankful in all things. Let me share a story with you.

When our son was a student in the seminary, he had to have knee surgery because of a basketball injury. "Simple, minor surgery," we were told. However, about a week or so later we received a telephone call early one morning from the head nurse of the intensive care unit of a major hospital. I will never forget her words: "Your son is in the hospital with septicemia (blood poisoning) and a severe staphylococcal infection in his operative knee. It looks like we are going to have to put him on a respirator because he is having rapid, difficult breathing. You may want to get here as quickly as you can."

Immediately my husband and I dropped to our knees in prayer. Our prayer went something like this, "Father, Keith is Your child. You gave him to us to rear. We know You want what is best for him. We thank You because we know You are in charge of even this. All we ask is that Your will be done with our son."

We got up from our knees and woke up his sisters to get ready for our trip to be by his side. Then the phone rang again. The nurse from the hospital called again. She said she was not sure what just happened but for some "unexplained" reason, our son's breathing returned to normal. He no longer needed the respirator. Tears of joy flooded my soul. What can I say? Answered prayer or thankful prayer or both—our Heavenly Father had more things for our son to do! In fact, God used this experience to change his view of life. PTL, it changed our lives, too!

♥ **Read Philippians 4:6-7. How do you respond to what Paul is telling you to do?**

_____

_____

These are some of my very favorite Scripture verses. I even had the words embroidered as my daily reminder not to worry about anything but instead to pray about everything and to thank Him for all the things He has done. I know if I abide by these words, I will experience God's peace, which is far more wonderful than the human mind can understand. Our Heavenly Father's peace guards our hearts and minds as we live in Jesus. For a *faith that works*, be willing to be cheerful and praise and thank your Holy God in all situations, including suffering. What about you? Do you pray about everything? Do you thank God in all things—even the sufferings you may experience? I hope so; doing this will change your life!

---♥ ---
I have never stopped thanking God for you, I pray for you constantly.
(Eph. 1:16).

Your Thoughts

Questions

Comments

Prayer Requests

Prayer Answers

Week 9, Day 2

Prayers for the Sick

Today's Focus: James 5:14-15; 1 Peter 5:1-4; 1 John 1:9; 5:14-15; Matthew 17:20; Luke 10:30-37; John 9:2-3; 14:13-14; Mark 2:1-12; 2 Corinthians 12:7-9; Colossians 1:3, 9-11; 1 Samuel 16:1-13

> **† Heart Truths:**
>
> *Is anyone among you sick? Let him call for the elders of the church, and let them pray over him, anointing him with oil in the name of the Lord; and the prayer offered in faith will restore the one who is sick . . .* (Jas. 5:14-15a NAS).

Today most believers recognize we are to pray or intercede for those who are sick. In fact praying for the sick is one of the characteristics of our churches as it was in the days of James. But do we have a specific way we are to pray when folks are sick? *Intercession*—what is it?

The Biblical Cyclopedic Index defines *intercession* as the prayers offered on the behalf of others. Perhaps it means to plead or petition another person's case for favors such as mercy or healing. Of course when we petition in prayer, we go to a higher authority; that authority is our Heavenly Father. As believers we are commanded to pray not only for ourselves but for other people . . . especially for other believers. But as we studied yesterday, pray for yourself first to have your sins forgiven and have restored fellowship with our Holy God. We have the assurance that God will forgive our sins and cleanse us from all unrighteousness (1 John 1:9). After we are cleansed, then we are able to intercede on behalf of others with our Heavenly Father. Why is James so specific on how to go about praying for those who are sick? Let's see how his instructions affect our intercession today.

♥ Read James 5:14-15. How do you respond to the specific instructions that James gives on how to pray for those who are sick?

_____

_____

James instructs people who are sick to call for the church elders and have them pray over them. The elders are instructed to anoint the person with oil in the name of the Lord. James says that the prayers of the elders offered in faith will restore the sick person. Then James says the Lord will raise the sick person up and forgive any sins that may have been committed. Let's look at each of these instructions separately. First of all, let's study the call for the elders.

♥ **Read 1 Peter 5:1-4. Who do you consider to be the *elders*?**

_____

_____

♥ **Have you ever had an experience in which the elders or other mature Christian leaders prayed over you? If so, what happened?**

_____

_____

According to Peter the elders are spiritually mature leaders in the church who provide supervision, protection, discipline, instruction, and direction to the other believers. The word *elder* actually means *older*. The elders carry great responsibility as they lead the other believers by good example of godly living. They are to willingly care for God's flock and to serve faithfully with humility. In biblical days the church is a "lifestyle", not just a "Sunday-go-to-meeting day." In this context everyone knows everyone else; a real sense of community exists. Therefore, for the elders to be called to visit and pray for someone who is sick is quite normal. How I wish this were so today! Unfortunately many of us do not even know who our next-door neighbor is. By the way, be sure to notice who calls for the elders. That's right; the sick person is the one who makes the call. Read further.

♥ **Read John 14:13-14. In what way do you think the elders are to pray?**

_____

_____

Jesus tells us that whatever we ask in His name, He will do. What does praying in the "name of Jesus" mean? It means we are to genuinely seek to ask in accordance with God's will and to be obedient to His commands. This does not mean that Jesus' name is a magic prescription to fulfill our self-seeking desires. When you pray, do you pray in the name of Jesus? Why or why not?

♥ **Read James 5:15. What else is involved in the elders' prayer?**

_____

_____

James tells us when we pray, we are to have faith and not to be doubtful. The elders are to have the faith that God will answer in accordance with His will. The faith of the sick person is not what matters; the faith of the elders does. How much faith is important to have? How much is enough faith? Jesus says if we only have the faith as small as a mustard seed, we can say for a mountain to move to another place and it would get up and move. Nothing would be impossible! (Mt. 17:20) The size of a mustard seed is not very big. Is Jesus saying our prayers do not really depend on the size of our faith but instead on our trust and dependence on the power of God? I believe Jesus is telling us that a prayer offered in faith means we have the faith that believes God can heal as well as the faith that expresses our complete confidence in His will. As you know, God is sovereign; His will is absolute.

♥ Why do you think some believers are reluctant to pray to God for healing?

_____

_____

♥ Have you ever been reluctant to pray to God for healing? Please explain.

_____

_____

Perhaps some believers are reluctant to pray for healing for fear their prayers will not be granted in the way they want them granted. Sometimes I wonder why we think we can dictate our desires to our Heavenly Father. We know exactly how we want Him to answer our prayers. If He doesn't, we think we should "excuse" Him. Excuse me! Who do we think we are? Do we trust God only as long as He cooperates with our plans? If so, that is no trust at all! True prayer gives God the freedom to work according to His will and not according to ours. Perhaps we need to have an eternal point of view. That is one reason I pray to be able to see with His eyes, to hear with His ears, and to speak with His mouth. My own viewpoint is way too limited! What about yours?

When we exaggerate the amount of faith that we are to have, we place too much emphasis on our ability to know God's plan about His answer to our prayer. However, if we have a small, simple faith that trusts in our holy Heavenly Father to do what is best, perhaps miracles will happen and our prayers will be heard (1 John 5:14-15). After all, the Lord is the One who heals; our faith is not what heals. God's will is final (2 Cor. 12:7-9).

♥ Read Luke 10:30-37. Why do you think the elders are instructed to anoint the sick person with oil?

_____

_____

For some reason being anointed with oil really bothers some believers. Let's talk about it. First of all, James refers to someone who is physically ill and not just to anyone. As you know, in the Bible story, oil is used both as a medicine (Luke 10:30-37) and as a symbol of God's Spirit (1 Sam. 16:1-13). The Good Samaritan anoints the wounded man with oil; Samuel anoints David with oil to set him apart to be king. Therefore, oil represents both the physical and the spiritual. However, today many believers try to separate the physical from the spiritual. Think about it. Who is Lord over both your body and your spirit? Perhaps we should not try and separate the two. I often wonder whether we would see more healings take place if we anointed the sick person with oil.

♥ Read Mark 2:1-12 and John 9:2-3. How do you respond to what these verses claim can be the cause of illness?

_____

_____

In Mark we see Jesus forgiving the paralyzed man of his sins before healing his body. However, in John we learn that sin is not always the cause of our illness. Instead Jesus says the man's blindness occurs so the power of God can be seen in him. Only God can judge a person's true heart and knows the reason for someone's illness. But that does not excuse us from praying for someone's healing. Always pray, especially for other believers.

♥ Read Colossians 1:3, 9-11. After you read these verses, decide how you are to pray for other believers. Write your answer here.

_____

_____

How do we pray for our church leaders and our missionaries? How do we pray for believers we have never met? How do we pray for each other? Paul instructs us to first thank God for their faith and changed lives. Then he tells us to ask our Father to help them know His will, grant them spiritual understanding and wisdom, help them be willing to live for Him, help them know God better every day, give them patience and strength to endure what occurs in their lives, fill them with joy and thankfulness, and keep them safe at all times.

According to James a prayer offered in faith will restore the one who is sick; any-one who has committed sins will be forgiven (Jas. 5:15). Tomorrow, we will dis-cuss about the prayer component of confession. However, we actually have no choice about our intercession for others. To have a _faith that works_, intercede in prayer for your fellow believers, sick or not. Your responsibility does not stop there; also intercede for your spiritual leaders, rulers, neighbors, family, friends, and even your enemies. Let your prayer connect those in need with the all-powerful God of the universe. Only He knows what is best for each of us. May our Heavenly Father forgive us if we fail to do so!

-- ♥ --

Observe that the saving of the sick is not ascribed to the anointing with oil, but to prayer. In a time of sickness it is not cold and formal prayer that is effectual, but the prayer of faith.

Matthew Henry

More things are wrought by prayer, than this world dreams of.

Tennyson

Your Thoughts

Questions

Comments

Prayer Requests

Prayer Answers

Week 9, Day 3

Prayers of Confession

Today's Focus: James 5:16; 1 John 1:9; Psalms 32:1-5; 51:1-19; 1 Peter 2:9; 1 Chronicles 21:8; Nehemiah 9:2-3

Let everyone who enjoys confessing your sins to other people please stand up. OK, now that we are all seated . . . *hmmm*, guess most of us are human. Putting all foolishness aside, confession is downright painful! Why do you suppose that is true? Could this be because confession makes us feel so shameful, guilty, and vulnerable? Confessing our sins to our Heavenly Father is one thing; sharing those same sins with other people is quite different. Not all of us has a best friend we would trust not to betray us if we told all. Most of us have a deep need for acceptance; we do not want people to think badly of us nor look down on us. So instead we put on a front that makes others think we are perfect.

Satan loves secrets; he is the one who tells us we ought not to confess our sins for such reasons as just mentioned. Then when we do, Satan makes us have this overwhelming guilt. In place of confession we tend to put on masks. Some of us put on clown masks, because laughter seems to soften our uncomfortable feelings and insecurities. Have you ever made light of something painful? Have you refused to share with someone because you were afraid of that person's reaction to your sin? Have you ever kept quiet on a subject because you thought it would make you look bad? Does any of this apply to you? Maybe I am the only guilty party here, but I don't think so. May God help us and even encourage us to be transparent with each other. Let's see what God's Word has to say.

♥ **Read James 5:16. How did you respond to the commands this verse gives?**

_____

_____

♥ **Why do you think James gives these commands?**

_____

_____

Our Heavenly Father makes our approaching Him directly through the death, burial, and resurrection of our Lord Jesus possible. However, this does not excuse us from confessing our sins to each other. James does not say to confess our sins to each other if we want to. He says to do it; it is a command, not a choice. Why? James says it is so we may be healed and can accomplish much. But how does confession heal and accomplish much? Let's see.

♥ **How do you define** *confession?*

_____

_____

♥ **Read 1 John 1:9. What does God do when you confess your sins?**

_____

_____

To confess is to agree with God that what we have done is sinful and our desire to do the sin is wrong. What are the results of confession? According to 1 John if we confess our sins, God is faithful and just to forgive us of our sins and to cleanse us from all wrong. Your Heavenly Father forgives you! Forgiveness is an act of pardon; actually it is a new lease on life. Forgiveness is awesome, because it is cleansing and freeing. You are released and freed from the burden of your sin. You once again are able to enjoy the fellowship with Jesus and your Heavenly Father. Your entire being is lighter.

Our Heavenly Father wants and desires to forgive us. His only beloved Son died so He could offer us pardon for our sins. But first confess your sins to receive that forgiveness and enjoy total fellowship with Him. Deep, heartfelt, true confession involves a commitment not to continue with the sin we are confessing. The same is true when we confess our sins to other believers. If you have sinned against someone, ask for that person's forgiveness. If our sins have affected other members of the body, we must confess it publicly. Believe it or not, every believer is a priest to other believers (1 Pet. 2:9). Therefore, each of us has the responsibility to forgive others. Sometimes we say we have forgiven others, but instead, we bury the hatchet with the handle exposed. I encourage you to break off that handle and bury the hatchet so it can never be found again. That is what true forgiveness really is. What do you think? How does confession play a role in all of this?

♥ **Read Psalms 51. How do you respond to what these verses teach you about confession?**

_____

_____

In this psalm David pleads for mercy, forgiveness, and cleansing from God. David immediately confesses his sin and demonstrates real sorrow about it. One of the most important characteristics of true confession is that we are really sorry for what we have done. David asks God to forgive him, to purify him, and to wash him so he will be clean once again. David believes God has heard him and will restore him by creating a clean heart within him.

We, too, can admit our sins, be truly sorry for our actions, and ask God to cleanse us from our sins and restore us to fellowship and service. We also can believe God will do what He promises to do. Sin hurts! It not only hurts us and others, but it hurts our Heavenly Father. Sin in any shape or form is rebellion against our Father's ways of living. Confess it readily. According to God's Word confession precedes forgiveness (1 Chron. 21:8) and worship (Neh. 9:2-3). When we read and study the Holy Bible, our Father reveals our sins to us. This convicts us to confess them. However, if we hang on to certain sins, we cannot have a right relationship with God. Our Heavenly Father tells us to worship Him in spirit and in truth. To experience true worship, go through the entire process of confession, forgiveness, and restoration.

♥ **From the following verses, identify what you believe to be the results of true confession.**

Psalms 32:1-5

_____

Psalms 51:12-19

_____

James 5:16

_____

When we confess our sins, this opens the way for our Heavenly Father to bring good out of bad situations. True confession results in forgiveness, pardon, renewed fellowship, healing, and even greater accomplishments. How awesome is that! Confession to other believers brings about the same results. Our fellowship is restored; we are forgiven and pardoned; we are healed spiritually, emotionally, and maybe even physically; and we are freed to accomplish greater things. But not only are we to confess our sins to each other, we also are to pray for each other.

How many times have you witnessed broken fellowship in a church because some-one held a grudge against someone else? Or, you experience some kind of unre-solved anger or resentment or bitterness. Perhaps you even know of a lack of for-giveness. You may have seen someone avoiding another person and sitting on the opposite side of the church. All of these things cause real disunity in the body of believers and even may lead to physical ailments. If believers would freely confess their sins to those they have wronged, and if need be, confess them publicly so the church could pray for the person, then barriers would be torn down and real healing would occur. God calls for the church to be of one mind and one body and to be unified, not broken. The prayer of believers is the most powerful source of communication we have with our Heavenly Father. Through this media, healing and forgiveness occurs. It is the weapon against the evil one. To have victory in a *faith that works*, pray faithfully. Confession is part of those prayers.

--♥ --

When we acknowledge our faults to each other, it will lead greatly to peace and brotherly love.

Matthew Henry

Forgiveness is freedom from your past because it no longer has the power to hurt you.

Anonymous

Your Thoughts

Questions

Comments

Prayer Requests

Prayer Answers

Week 9, Day 4

Power of Prayer

† Heart Truths:

Elijah was a man with a nature like ours, and he prayed earnestly that it might not rain; and it did not rain on the earth for three years and six months (Jas. 5:17 NAS).

Today's Focus: James 5:17-18; 1 Kings 17:1-7; 18:20-45; Isaiah 55:8-9; Jeremiah 33:3; Matthew 19:26; 1 Timothy 2:1-4

For the past three days we have studied about prayer. We have examined praise, thanksgiving, confession, and intercession and connected these components with suffering, healing, and forgiveness. Today we are connecting these components to the power of prayer that our Heavenly Father desires for us to have. Since God's power is considerably greater than ours is, wouldn't totally depending on Him make sense for us? After all, don't we have a God Who makes the impossible become possible? (Mt. 19:26). Why then are we so hesitant to surrender to His power and allow Him to use it in and through us? Prayer is our most powerful source of communication with our holy Heavenly Father. Have you been awed lately by the power of prayer? If not, why not? Are you missing one of the greatest blessings that God bestows on His children? Let's see why James uses the example of Elijah.

♥ **Read 1 Kings 17:1-7 and 18:20-45. Answer the following questions.**

For what does Elijah pray?

_____

_____

Why do you think this happens?

_____

_____

How does God answer Elijah's prayers?

_____

_____

What takes place on Mount Carmel?

_____

_____

What are the lessons you learned from the above incidents?

_____

_____

As you know from the Bible story, Elijah is a famous prophet who has an intimate, personal relationship with God. He believes and has confidence that God will answer his prayers. Elijah is best known for two incidents: praying for the beginning and end of a three-year drought and representing God in a confrontation with the priests of Baal. We observe Elijah boldly walking into the presence of Ahab, a Baal-worshipping king, and telling him rain will not fall for several years. Then three years later he returns to Ahab and announces that rain will fall soon, even though the famine by that time is extremely severe. Wow! What a manifestation of the authority of our Heavenly Father!

In the confrontation with the priests of Baal, Elijah issues a challenge to the people to take a stand to follow whoever is the "True God." I am amused to picture those 450 Baal priests shouting and dancing around wildly and trying to get the attention of their god and having no results. I can almost join Elijah as he mocks them and tells them to shout louder because their god must be asleep. How sad to read that the priests even cut themselves to get Baal's attention! Then Elijah calls the people to build an altar, place the bull on it, and drench it with water three times. At the customary time of the evening sacrifice, Elijah simply walks around the altar and prays. Immediately the Lord answers his prayer by burning up the bull on the altar along with all the surrounding water in the ditch. Wow! What a demonstration of God's power! After that awesome demonstration Elijah goes up to Mount Carmel and prays for rain. Folks, as we pray, we can have the faith that whatever our Heavenly Father tells us to do, He will provide the means to carry it through.

♥ Read James 5:17-18. According to these verses what kind of nature do you think Elijah has?

_____

_____

♥ What kind of nature do you have?

_____

James says that Elijah has a nature like ours. Why do you think James tells us that? Could one reason be because Elijah flees in fear from Jezebel immediately after the confrontation with the priests of Baal? After all, she does threaten his life. Before you criticize him, put yourself in his place. What would you have done? Fear is a very human response. Have you ever been afraid of something? When does Satan close in on us with an attack? Doesn't this happen immediately after our moments of greatest victories or when we are "up on the mountaintop" spiritually? Of course it is. Could another reason be that at times Elijah feels all alone and isolated? But God reassures him 7,000 other believers exist. God even sends ravens to care and feed Elijah.

Have you ever felt isolated and alone? I sure have at times. Feeling all alone is also a very human response. Just remember our Heavenly Father is always there. From Scripture, we also know God speaks to Elijah in a gentle whisper and not in the windstorm or the earthquake or the fire. Does that mean we need to be quiet and listen as we approach Him in our prayers? Listen! Is He speaking even now? Our Heavenly Father often speaks through the gentle whisper rather than raging and extravagant elements of nature. Now that we have observed the never-ending power of Elijah's prayer, we can realize that same power is available to you and me today.

♥ **Read Jeremiah 33:3. What do you think you need to do to receive God's power in prayer?**

_____

_____

The more we pray with faith and in God's will, the more we see our Heavenly Father answering our prayers. The more we see Him answering our prayers, the stronger our faith becomes. When we have many experiences of answered prayer on which we can build our faith, doubts flee. We no longer are tossed about with a doubtful mind (Jas. 1:6). But, ask first! Jeremiah says to ask and God will show us great and mighty things we do not know. Read on.

♥ **Read Isaiah 55:8-9. How do you know you can trust God's ways and thoughts?**

_____

_____

God's thoughts are different from ours. His ways are far greater than anything we could ever imagine. His ways and thoughts are so much higher than our ways and thoughts. Sometimes we foolishly try to make God's plans conform to our plans rather than us conforming to His plans. According to Henry Blackaby we are to see where God is working and join Him. Remember, with God all things are possible (Mt. 19:26). I do not want to even think of having a life without Him. I know I would not survive. What about you?

♥ Read 1 Timothy 2:1-4. In these verses for what are you instructed to pray?

_____

Even though our Heavenly Father is all-powerful and all-knowing and His ways and thoughts are much higher than ours, He has chosen us to change the world through our prayers. Therefore, constantly pray for all people—for kings and those in authority, as well as for everyone to be saved and know the truth. Prayer is the key that unlocks the *faith that works* in our lives. The power of prayer is proved from the life of Elijah. For you to have effective, powerful prayers, ask with an humble spirit and a mindset of total dependence on our Heavenly Father. Prayer reveals our faith and dependence on God as we ask Him to fill us with His power. You cannot replace prayer with anything else; nothing is comparable, especially when you think of impossible circumstances. What about you? Do you have power in your prayers? Are you experiencing answered prayers? You'll find no greater joy.

---♥ ---

Prayer is the Christian's lifeline to God, and with it lives are changed for eternity!

Charles H. Spurgeon

In prayer we must not look to our own merit, but to the grace of God. It is not enough to just say a prayer; we must pray in prayer. Thoughts must be fixed, desires must be firm and fervent, and graces exercised. The power of prayer encourages every believer to be sincere in prayer.

Matthew Henry

Your Thoughts

Questions

Comments

Prayer Requests

Prayer Answers

208

Week 9, Day 5

Confronting Believers

Today's Focus: James 5:19-20; Matthew 18:15-17; Galatians 2:11-13; 1 Corinthians 5:1-13; 1 John 5:16; 2 Thessalonians 3:14-15; 1 Peter 4:8; 2 Corinthians 2:4-8; 7:4-15; 8:21; 10:2-13; 11:22-27; 12:14-19; 13:2-13; Proverbs 10:12; Ezekiel 3:18-21; 33:9; Romans 3:23; John 3:16; Acts 16:31; Ephesians 2:9; 4:26

Confrontation: some of us run from it; some of us run toward it and may even enjoy it. During our earlier years of marriage my husband accused me of really enjoying confrontation, but as the years passed, he realized that I did not like it, let alone enjoy it. In fact confrontation gives me the jitters and all sorts of physical ailments when I have to do it. I take my Heavenly Father literally when He tells me not to let the sun go down on my anger (Eph. 4:26). When I was growing up, I had a father and mother who would get so angry with each other that the words would fly followed by weeks of dead silence. Unfortunately, I became the "go-between" and was forced to tell them what each other said. I heard commands, such as, "Tell your mama." I knew that wasn't right and vowed some day when I had a family of my own to always discuss things, no matter how long this took or how painful this became. So, when our marriage was blessed with children, we had family conferences to discuss a problem or disagreement or misbehavior that affected all of us. Pleasant? No, not at all, but necessary. The joy of reconciliation and forgiveness that followed was worth the struggle of dealing with whatever had happened. The same is true when we see a believing brother or sister stray. Deal with that person immediately. According to James that person's sin will be forgiven and everyone will be blessed. Let's read God's Word and understand the biblical way to confront others.

♥ Read James 5:19-20. How do you respond to the one James mentions in this passage?

_____

James says that if anyone among us strays away from the truth and is brought back again, the one who brings the sinner back will save that person from death and bring about the forgiveness of many sins. In these verses the one who strays is another believer who has turned from the central truth that Jesus is the Son of God,

Who died for ours sins, rose again, and is our Lord and Savior. This person evidently has made choices and actions toward denying the Lordship of Jesus and no longer lives a life consistent with Christian beliefs. In this passage *death* is not necessarily referring to physical death but to spiritual death. Whether you believe a person can lose his or her salvation is not the issue here. Instead the main issue is to agree that if a person strays away from the faith, the person is in severe trouble and needs to repent and be brought back. Does that mean we have a responsibility to our fellow believers? You better believe it does! We are not asked whether we want to; we are commanded to confront the person who strays (1 Cor. 5:1-2). Why do you think the Scripture indicates for us to confront other believers? What does "tolerated" sin do to a fellowship of believers? It can destroy it; remember, sin is like a cancer. People like to have others join with them in their sin. So not only will it have an effect on the sinner but on others as well. Let's look at an example.

♥ **Read Galatians 2:11-13. Why do you think Paul confronts Peter?**

_____

_____

Even though Peter is a leader of the church, he is acting like a hypocrite. Peter has joined the Judaizers and is supporting their claim that Jesus is not sufficient for salvation. He may have also been thinking that by his staying away from the Gentiles he would keep from offending James and the Jewish Christians. (As you know, James presides over the Jerusalem council.) However, Peter is driven by fear of what James and the others will think. Consequently, Paul believes Peter's actions violate true Christian beliefs. He confronts Peter before his actions damage the church. So Paul publicly opposes Peter face to face. Never compromise the truth of God's Word, because to do so places us and others on a slippery slope. All of us—even church leaders—make mistakes. Perhaps another believer may need to get someone back on the right track. So how do we do it? What is the biblical way of confrontation?

♥ **Read the following verses. Identify how you are to prepare before you confront others.**

1 John 5:16

_____

2 Corinthians 2:4

_____

Proverbs 10:12

_____

210

The first thing to do if you see another believer sinning is to pray for that person. However, also pray for yourself to have the right words to say. Ask your Heavenly Father to provide the right time and place for the confrontation and to go ahead of you to prepare the heart of the person involved in the sin. The other thing to do is to show genuine love for that person. According to Proverbs and 1 Peter we show deep love for each other because "love covers a multitude of sin." But how do we show that love? I believe we should share our concerns honestly and with the right heart attitude in hopes the person will repent and return from straying. So how do we go about it? As you may know, we can find right and wrong approaches when we confront others. Let's look first at what <u>NOT</u> to do.

♥ **Have you had an experience in which you or someone close to you was confronted in the wrong way? What happened?**

_____

_____

♥ **What do you think might be the wrong way to confront someone?**

_____

_____

True love means that sometimes we confront those about whom we care the most. Even though love covers a multitude of sins, we still can go about confrontation all wrong. This would further break relationships rather than heal them. Sometimes we can be too legalistic and condemn the person with the laws that we think they should have obeyed and not broken. Sometimes we can ignore this and pretend the situation doesn't exist because we do not want to deal with it. Sometimes we can isolate the person and with our gossiping turn others against him or her. Sometimes we can accuse the person to the point of making the individual defensive and driving him or her further away. You've heard people say that when you point a finger at someone, three fingers point back at yourself. So what is the right and best approach to confrontation?

♥ **What do you think is the right way to confront someone?**

_____

_____

After examining the wrong approach to confrontation, let's examine the right approach. In 2 Corinthians we see some basic principles we can use when we confront someone. According to these verses when we confront a person we are to—

Approach	2 Corinthians
• Be bold and firm	7:9, 10:2
• Affirm the good you see in the person	7:4
• Be honest and accurate	7:14; 8:21
• Know all the facts	11:22-27
• After confronting, follow up	7:13; 12:14
• Be gentle after being firm	7:15; 13:11-13
• Speak Jesus' words, not your own	10:4, 12, 13; 12:19
• Use church discipline as last resort	13:2

Now that we have examined the right and wrong approach to confrontation, let's identify the proper steps to take to bring a straying brother or sister back to the truth. Using the right approach as we go through these steps is important; after all repentance and forgiveness and not vengeance are what we seek for them! Let's see what Jesus says to do to restore that person.

♥ **Read Matthew 18:15-17. After you read these verses, describe the steps you believe Jesus says we are to follow when we confront a believer who sins.**

_____

_____

Jesus gives us specific guidelines for dealing with believers who sin. Even though Jesus is primarily talking about another believer who sins against us, these guide-lines also apply to other situations involving members of the church family. Jesus' words are not an excuse to use the wrong approach on any person who hurts us. Nor are Jesus' words an authorization to gossip or call for a church examination. Jesus' words are designed to reconcile the one who strays, to cause repentance and forgiveness, and to enable the believers to live in harmony and unity.

The first thing Jesus tells us to do is to be direct. We are to go to the believer pri-vately and point out the problem. If the person listens and confesses it, we have won that person back. If not we are to take one or two other believers with us and go back again to the person who has strayed. If the person still refuses to listen, then we take the case to the church and let the church members decide what is right or wrong. If the person still refuses to accept the rebuke, Jesus says to treat him or her as a pagan.

Paul takes church discipline a step further. Paul says to remove the person from the fellowship of the church (1 Cor. 5:2-13). But remember, if the person chooses to repent, then give forgiveness and comfort (2 Cor. 2:5-8). If no repentance occurs, we are not to associate with the disobedient person. If we speak to the person, we must only do so in a manner in which to issue a warning (2 Thess. 3:14,15). Paul further states that after two warnings, the person is to be removed from the fellowship (Titus 3:10). But a word of warning: never be unforgiving as you are hoping to bring the person back to repentance and restoration.

Why are we not following Jesus' advice about discipline and confrontation in our churches today? Have we become so numb and tolerant to sin we are willing to overlook almost anything? Do you know of a problem affecting your church which everyone would benefit from dealing with? If so, why has it been ignored? Could this be part of our problem today? Do we not realize a church that does not discipline blatant sin among the members causes a division and paralyzes the effectiveness of the church? What about confrontation with unbelievers?

♥ **Read Ezekiel 3:18-21 and 33:9. What do you think is your responsibility toward unbelievers?**

_____

_____

Actually believers are commanded and have a unique responsibility to warn unbelievers of the consequences of rejecting God and Jesus. If we fail to do this, our Heavenly Father holds us responsible for what happens to them. OUCH! If nothing else this can motivate us to share our faith in both word and deed boldly with unbelievers. We are told that if we warn them to repent and they do not repent, then they will die in their sins, but we will not be held responsible. Folks, as believers, we have only one thing we are to share with the unbelievers; that is the gospel of our Lord Jesus Christ. We are not to force our Christian standards on them nor confuse them by getting them to believe that to be a Christian, they must do certain things. Our only responsibility with unbelievers is to share our testimony that we are all sinners (Rom. 3:23); a lost person can do nothing to save himself or herself (Eph. 2:9); Jesus was born, crucified, buried, and resurrected to save the lost person from his or her sin (John 3:16); to be saved the lost person must believe God's Word, repent of the sin, and invite Jesus into his or her heart by faith (Acts 16:31). Then the angels will rejoice with you when a new believer is born!

Keep in mind as we associate with unbelievers, we have to keep a close watch on ourselves and on our teachings from God's Word. Stay true to what is right so our Heavenly Father will save us and those who hear us (1 Tim. 4:16). We have to be careful to stay on guard against those who may try to lead us into sin. A _faith that works_ is a faith that confronts a straying believer as well as confronts an unbeliever who needs Jesus. By taking the right approach, praying for the person, and acting in love, we can meet the person where he or she is and bring that person back to our Heavenly Father to receive forgiveness.

As we conclude our study, we recognize that the Book of James is a practical guide for Christian living. It is a book that literally teaches us how to have a *faith that works* in our everyday lives. We have discovered that faith takes us through troubles, doubts, and temptations. As we have immersed ourselves in each faith characteristic, we have determined that a *faith that works* obeys God's Word, removes partiality, confirms itself by action, controls the tongue, and produces wisdom, humility, and trust in God. If we trust and obey our Heavenly Father while we wait patiently and pray faithfully, we know we can look forward with confidence to the return of our Lord Jesus. As believers let us love and serve others as we live out God's principles in the world.

--♥--

Faith never knows where it is being led, but it loves and knows the ONE who is leading.

Oswald Chambers

Your Thoughts

Questions

Comments

Prayer Requests

Prayer Answers

Closing Letter to Readers

Dearest Precious Friends,

Developing this study truly has been an awesome experience for me. Our Father has taught me so very much and has further sealed some biblical principles in my life. I pray our Heavenly Father has spoken to you, too, through His Word as you have studied this remarkable Book of James. I also pray you have grown at least one step higher in your relationship with our Father because of your perseverance, involvement, and commitment.

Thank you for walking with me through the Book of James. May you continue to hide His words in your heart as you in the days ahead put your faith into action! May our Heavenly Father BLESS you abundantly and always hold you in the palm of His hand.

Do keep in touch. Perhaps you can let me know how this study may have affected your life. My joy has been to serve you.

Love and prayers,

Anne

Philippians 4:6-7

Translations

This Bible study uses several different translations because I believe comparing translations is important and helpful. This enables us to have a fresh look at God's Truth and encourages us to dig deeper to understand the meaning. Therefore, throughout the study I have used the abbreviated short forms listed below to identify Scripture quotations and paraphrases.

Unless otherwise indicated Scripture quotations are from—

NLT   *New Living Translation*
           Wheaton, IL: Tyndale House Publishers (1996)

Other translations

Msg   *The Message*
           Colorado Springs: Navpress (1995)

NAS   *New American Standard Bible*
           New York: Thomas Nelson Publishers (1985)

NIV   *New International Version*
           Colorado Springs: International Bible Society (1999)

NKJ   *New King James Bible*
           New York: Thomas Nelson Publishers (1983)

LB   *Living Bible*
           Wheaton, IL: Tyndale House Publishers (1979)

Bibliography

Antiquities of the Jews, Complete Works of Josephus, The Chronology of Biblical Christianity, (20). The Bible Library Suite CD. Ellis Enterprises, 2000.

Bamford's Bible Dictionary. The Bible Library Suite CD. Ellis Enterprises, 2000.

Barton, Bruce B., Veerman, David R., Wilson, Neil. *Life Application Bible Commentary.* James. Wheaton, IL: Tyndale House Publishers, 1992.

Biblical Cyclopedic Index. Open Bible, (Expanded Edition), New American Standard Version. NY: Thomas Nelson Publishers, 1985.

Briscoe, Jill. *8 Choices That Will Change a Woman's Life.* Monroe, LA: Howard Publishing, 2004.

Chambers, Oswald. *My Utmost for His Highest.* NY: Dodd, Mead & Company, 1963.

Cowman, Mrs. Charles. *Streams in the Desert.* Grand Rapids, MI: Daybreak Books, Zondervan,1965.

Cymbala, Jim. *Fresh Faith.* Grand Rapids, MI: Zondervan, 1999.

Easton's Bible Dictionary. The Bible Library Suite CD, Ellis Enterprises, 2000.

Gray's Home Bible Commentary. The Bible Library Suite CD, Ellis Enterprises, 2000.

Henry, Matthew. *Concise Commentary: James.* The Bible Library Suite CD. Ellis Enterprises, 2000.

Life Application Dictionary/Concordance. New Living Translation. Wheaton, IL: Tyndale House Publishers, 1996.

Lucado, Max. *Grace for the Moment.* Nashville, TN: Countryman, 2000.

Strong's Greek New Testament Dictionary. The Bible Library Suite CD, Ellis Enterprises, 2000.

Torrey, R. A. *Torrey's New Topical Textbook.* The Bible Library Suite CD. Ellis Enterprises, 2000.

Warren, Rick. *The Purpose Driven Life: What on Earth Am I Here For?* Grand Rapids, MI: Zondervan, 2002.

Wilson, Mimi & Volkhardt, Shelly Cook. *Holy Habits: A Woman's Guide to Intentional Living.* Colorado Springs, CO: Navpress, 1999.

Appendix

Chart 1: Comparing James to the Sermon on the Mount
(accompanies Introduction/Overview)

TOPIC	JAMES	MATTHEW
Troubles and persecution	1:2	5:10-12
Endurance	1:4	5:48
Ask God; He answers	1:5; 5:15	7:7-12
Poor people	1:9	5:3
Anger can be dangerous	1:20	5:22
Be merciful to others	2:13	5:7; 6:14
Faith proven by actions	2:14-16	7:21-23
Recognizing fruit in peoples' lives	2:18; 3:12	7:16-17
Peacemakers	3:17, 18	5:9
Friendship with evil, enemy of God	4:4	6:24
Humble yourself; He will encourage you	4:10	5:3-4
Don't criticize or speak evil of others	4:11	7:1-2
Treasures on earth erode	5:2-3	6:19
Patient in suffering	5:10	5:12
Honest in speech	5:12	5:33-37

Chart 2: The Two Perspectives of James and Paul
(accompanies Day 4 of Week 3, Faith Confirms Itself by Actions)

	JAMES	PAUL
JUSTIFIED	Refers to God's final judgment over the Christian life when a person is declared righteous for living a faithful life to the end	Refers to the "initial" granting of righteousness when a person accepts Jesus as Lord and Savior
WORKS/ ACTIONS	Refers to what a person does as the natural product of true faith	Refers to observing the law and what a person tries to do to be saved
	Expresses itself in actions	Expresses itself in love but actions follow
FAITH	States that faith alone is a shallow belief in an idea if no commitment or life change is involved	States that faith is a saving faith and is the belief that brings about an intimate union with Jesus and results in salvation and obedience
	Makes clear that God requires good deeds from those who are "in" the kingdom	Makes clear that a person "enters" into God's kingdom only by faith
	Concerned with "dead" faith	Concerned with "true" faith
	Emphasizes "post-salvation" results of a life of faith	Emphasizes the "beginning of salvation" is always faith, then actions follow (Gal. 5:6)

Chart 3: Earthly Wisdom versus Heavenly Wisdom
(accompanies Days 3 and 4 of Week 5, Faith Produces Wisdom)

	Earthly Unspiritual Wisdom	Heavenly Spiritual Wisdom
Source	Motivated by Satan	Granted by God
Motivation	Sinful desires	Desire to do God's will
Characteristics	Disorder and confusion	Order
	Bitter jealousy	Purity
	Selfish ambition	Peace
	All kinds of evil	Gentle and kind
	Manipulation	Loving and helping others
	Greed	Mercy
	Unspiritual thoughts and ideas	Good deeds
	Decreased morality	Impartial
	Prideful	Humility and sincerity
	Bragging	Just and fair
	Self-focus	Understanding
	Doing the wrong thing	Doing the right thing
		Knowledge
		Discernment
	Destructive competition	Eliminates need to compete with or compare ourselves to others
	Live in a way that leads to eternal death	Live in a way that leads to eternal life

Illustration 1: Who Is in Control?
(accompanies Day 4 of Week 4, Faith Controls the Tongue)

The circle below represents your life!
The throne in the center of the circle represents who controls your life.
Ask yourself these two questions:

1. Where is Jesus sitting in your life?
2. Is He sitting on the throne of your life or are you?
You have a choice! What will your choice be?

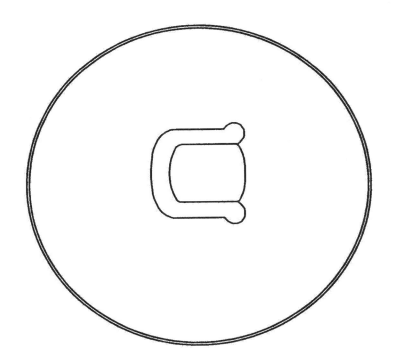

Illustration 2: The Vicious Cycle of Grumbling
(accompanies Day 2 of Week 8, Faith Waits Patiently)

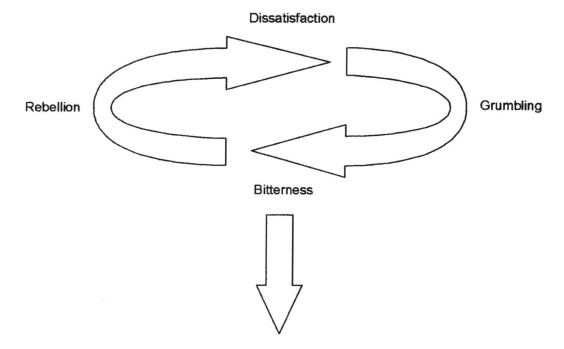

Dissatisfaction

Rebellion

Grumbling

Bitterness

Separation from God and Destruction

Evaluation

1. How well did the study of the Book of James help you apply a workable faith?

2. Did you experience any changes in your thoughts, attitudes, or behaviors? If so, please explain?

3. What benefit did you receive from studying James?

4. What areas of your life continue to challenge you? What do you plan to do about them?

5. Were you able to meet your expectations and/or goals for studying the Book of James?

6. What did you like best about this Bible study?

7. What did you like least about this Bible study?

8. What would you like to change about this Bible study?

9. What comments do you have about the group meetings?

10. What comments do you have about the facilitator of this study?

Thank you for your participation in the Bible study, *Faith that Works*. May our Father bless you abundantly!

Made in the USA
Lexington, KY
12 December 2014